B   McClard, Megan
Tub   Harriet Tubman -
             Slavery and the

DATE DUE

JAN 02 2008	

GAYLORD   PRINTED IN U.S.A.

GAYLORD

HARRIET TUBMAN

SLAVERY AND THE UNDERGROUND RAILROAD

THE HISTORY OF THE CIVIL WAR

CLARA BARTON: *Healing the Wounds*

JOHN C. CALHOUN *and the Roots of War*

JOHN ERICSSON *and the Inventions of War*

DAVID FARRAGUT *and the Great Naval Blockade*

ULYSSES S. GRANT *and the Strategy of Victory*

STONEWALL JACKSON: *Lee's Greatest Lieutenant*

ANDREW JOHNSON: *Rebuilding the Union*

ROBERT E. LEE *and the Rise of the South*

ABRAHAM LINCOLN: *To Preserve the Union*

HARRIET TUBMAN: *Slavery and the Underground Railroad*

THE HISTORY OF THE CIVIL WAR

HARRIET TUBMAN

SLAVERY AND THE UNDERGROUND RAILROAD

by MEGAN McCLARD

INTRODUCTORY ESSAY BY
HENRY STEELE COMMAGER

SILVER BURDETT PRESS

To Page Stickney

Series Editorial Supervisor: Richard G. Gallin
Series Editing: Agincourt Press
Series Consultant: Elizabeth Fortson
Cover and Text Design: Circa 86, New York
Series Supervision of Art and Design: Leslie Bauman
Maps: Susan Johnston Carlson

Consultants: Elysa Robinson, Detroit Board of Education, COMPACT
Coordinator; Karen E. Markoe, Professor of History, Maritime
College of the State University of New York.

Library of Congress Cataloging-in-Publication Data
McClard, Megan.
    Harriet Tubman : slavery and the underground railroad / by Megan
McClard.
        p.   cm. — (The History of the Civil War)
    Includes bibliograpical references (p. 126).
        Summary: A biography of the courageous woman who rose from slave
    beginnings to become a heroic figure in the Underground Railroad.
        1. Tubman, Harriet. 1820?–1913—Juvenile literature.   2. Slaves-
    -United States—Biography—Juvenile literature.   3. Afro-Americans-
    -Biography—Juvenile literature.   4. Underground railroad—Juvenile
    literature.   [1. Tubman, Harriet, 1820?–1913.   2. Afro-Americans-
    -Biography.   3. Underground railroad.]   I. Title.   II. Series
    E444.T82M37   1990
    305.5'67'092—dc20
    [B]
    [92]   90-32369
    ISBN 0-382-09938-9 (lib. bdg.)   ISBN 0-382-24047-2   CIP
                                                               AC

TABLE OF CONTENTS

Everyone in London travels the "Underground," just as everyone in New York City travels on the subway. Early in the last century, a very different kind of "underground" was operating in America. It was called the Underground Railroad, yet it was not a railroad and it was not underground. The only passengers on this "railroad" were blacks escaping from slavery in the South to freedom of the North, and even on to Canada, where there was no slavery.

How did they manage? Harriet Tubman, herself an ex-slave, would be the one to ask, if she were still alive today. Susan B. Anthony, who in her day had some claim to being the most effective champion of the emancipation of women, called Harriet Tubman the "most wonderful woman" she had ever known.

Wonderful she was. A slave herself, and married to a slave, she managed to escape from a farm on the eastern shore of Maryland, which was about as close to free territory as any other place in the Union. Once free, she devoted her energies and her wits—and she had a surplus of both—to helping others to escape.

Abolitionists in many states set up an "underground railroad" along which escaping slaves were passed from farmhouse to storage shed, from root cellar to barn until they reached safety in the North or in Canada. These hiding places along the way were known as "stations"—regular stops on the route to freedom.

In the course of her long life, a life often risked for the sake of others, Harriet Tubman managed to lead some 200 slaves to freedom. A female John Brown, Tubman never resorted to force, only to guide. No wonder she won the admiration of Brown himself, and of other prominent abolitionists such as William Lloyd Garrison and Theodore Parker.

Tubman, who became known as "General Tubman," did not give up her crusade once the war was over and the slaves "free at last." She busied herself setting up schools for black children.

Eventually she settled in upstate New York and in her old age became known as "Moses Tubman." She rejoiced in the name.

It is often said that the most influential woman of the Civil War era was Harriet Beecher Stowe, the author of *Uncle Tom's Cabin*. Tubman's contributions, while more direct, were no less important.

CIVIL WAR TIME LINE

May 22
Kansas-Nebraska Act states that in new territories the question of slavery will be decided by the citizens. Many Northerners are outraged because this act could lead to the extension of slavery.

1854	1855	1856	1857

May 21
Lawrence, Kansas is sacked by proslavery Missourians.
May 22
Senator Charles Sumner is caned by Preston Brooks for delivering a speech against slavery.
May 24 – 25
Pottawatomie Creek massacre committed by John Brown and four of his sons.

March 6
The Supreme Court, in the *Dred Scott* ruling, declares that blacks are not U. S. citizens, and therefore cannot bring lawsuits. The ruling divides the country on the question of the legal status of blacks.

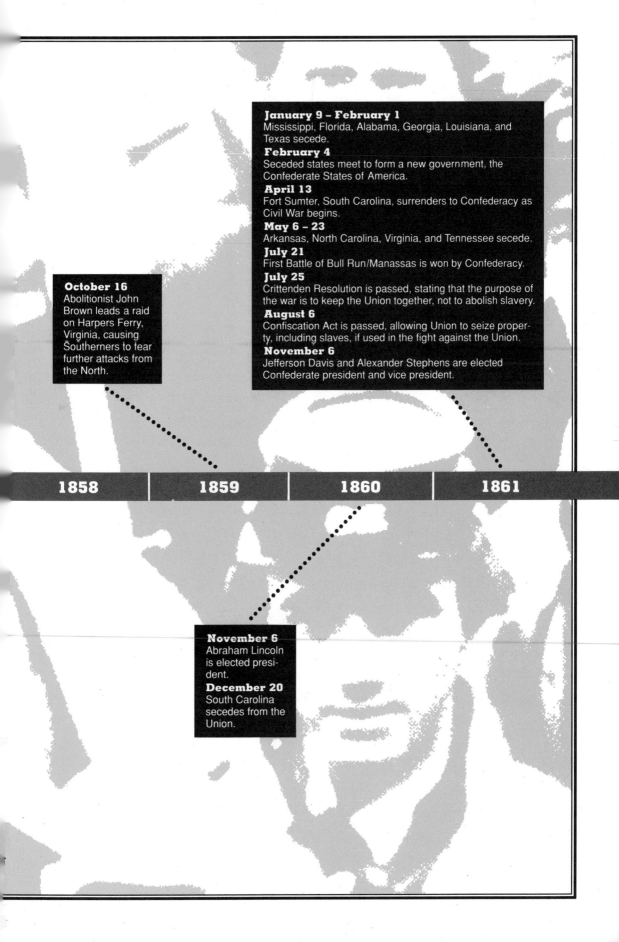

January 9 – February 1
Mississippi, Florida, Alabama, Georgia, Louisiana, and Texas secede.

February 4
Seceded states meet to form a new government, the Confederate States of America.

April 13
Fort Sumter, South Carolina, surrenders to Confederacy as Civil War begins.

May 6 – 23
Arkansas, North Carolina, Virginia, and Tennessee secede.

July 21
First Battle of Bull Run/Manassas is won by Confederacy.

July 25
Crittenden Resolution is passed, stating that the purpose of the war is to keep the Union together, not to abolish slavery.

August 6
Confiscation Act is passed, allowing Union to seize property, including slaves, if used in the fight against the Union.

November 6
Jefferson Davis and Alexander Stephens are elected Confederate president and vice president.

October 16
Abolitionist John Brown leads a raid on Harpers Ferry, Virginia, causing Southerners to fear further attacks from the North.

1858   **1859**   **1860**   **1861**

November 6
Abraham Lincoln is elected president.

December 20
South Carolina secedes from the Union.

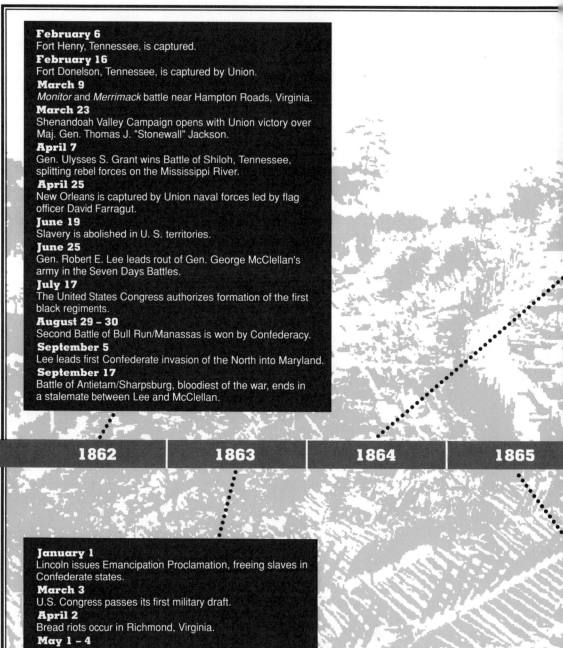

February 6
Fort Henry, Tennessee, is captured.

February 16
Fort Donelson, Tennessee, is captured by Union.

March 9
Monitor and *Merrimack* battle near Hampton Roads, Virginia.

March 23
Shenandoah Valley Campaign opens with Union victory over Maj. Gen. Thomas J. "Stonewall" Jackson.

April 7
Gen. Ulysses S. Grant wins Battle of Shiloh, Tennessee, splitting rebel forces on the Mississippi River.

April 25
New Orleans is captured by Union naval forces led by flag officer David Farragut.

June 19
Slavery is abolished in U. S. territories.

June 25
Gen. Robert E. Lee leads rout of Gen. George McClellan's army in the Seven Days Battles.

July 17
The United States Congress authorizes formation of the first black regiments.

August 29 – 30
Second Battle of Bull Run/Manassas is won by Confederacy.

September 5
Lee leads first Confederate invasion of the North into Maryland.

September 17
Battle of Antietam/Sharpsburg, bloodiest of the war, ends in a stalemate between Lee and McClellan.

1862 **1863** **1864** **1865**

January 1
Lincoln issues Emancipation Proclamation, freeing slaves in Confederate states.

March 3
U.S. Congress passes its first military draft.

April 2
Bread riots occur in Richmond, Virginia.

May 1 – 4
Battle of Chancellorsville is won by Confederacy; Stonewall Jackson is accidentally shot by his own troops.

May 22 – July 4
Union wins siege of Vicksburg in Mississippi.

June 3
Lee invades the North from Fredericksburg, Virginia.

July 3
Battle of Gettysburg is won in Pennsylvania by Union.

July 13 – 17
Riots occur in New York City over the draft.

November 19
Lincoln delivers the Gettysburg Address.

March 12
Grant becomes general-in-chief of Union army.
May 5 – 6
Lee and Lt. Gen. James Longstreet defeat Grant at the Wilderness Battle in Virginia.
May 6 – September 2
Atlanta Campaign ends in Union general William Tecumseh Sherman's occupation of Atlanta.
May 8 – 19
Lee and Grant maneuver for position in the Spotsylvania Campaign.
June 3
Grant is repelled at Cold Harbor, Virginia.
June 18, 1864 – April 2, 1865
Grant conducts the Siege of Petersburg, in Virginia, ending with evacuation of the city and Confederate withdrawal from Richmond.
August 5
Admiral Farragut wins Battle of Mobile Bay for Union.
October 6
Union general Philip Sheridan lays waste to Shenandoah Valley, Virginia, cutting off Confederacy's food supplies.
November 8
Lincoln is reelected president.
November 15 – December 13
Sherman's March to the Sea ends with Union occupation of Savannah, Georgia.

March 2
First Reconstruction Act is passed, reorganizing governments of Southern states.

| 1866 | 1867 | 1868 | 1869 |

April 9
Civil Rights Act of 1866 is passed. Among other things, it removes states' power to keep former slaves from testifying in court or owning property.

November 3
Ulysses S. Grant is elected president.

January 31
Thirteenth Amendment, freeing slaves, is passed by Congress and sent to states for ratification.
February 1 – April 26
Sherman invades the Carolinas.
February 6
Lee is appointed general-in-chief of Confederate armies.
March 3
Freedman's Bureau is established to assist former slaves.
April 9
Lee surrenders to Grant at Appomattox Courthouse, Virginia.
April 15
Lincoln dies from assassin's bullet; Andrew Johnson becomes president.
May 26
Remaining Confederate troops surrender.

HISTORY OF SLAVERY

"Slavery they can have anywhere. It is based on a weed that grows in every soil."

EDMUND BURKE

ven before Harriet Tubman was born, she had a powerful and evil enemy. Her enemy was not a person or even a country; it was the system known as chattel slavery. *Chattel* means property. Tubman, as well as her parents before her, was just that—someone else's property. It is known that at least two of her grandparents were captured by slave traders and brought to North America from the Slave Coast of Africa during the 18th century. Because slaves were not allowed to read and write, Tubman grew up illiterate. She left no letters or diaries that would later allow historians to piece together all the parts of her life story. But we do know that she was one of history's great heroes. With courage and determination, she escaped from slavery herself and then led more than 300 slaves to safety and freedom. When the Civil War began, she tirelessly scouted for the Union army and continued to free her people. Many of these newly freed slaves became new recruits for the Union army. Tubman rose from slavery to become one of the most important figures in the Civil War, and her story is certainly one of the most remarkable stories in the history of the United States of America.

Slavery did not begin in England or America. It had been practiced since ancient times by some of the most advanced societies. The ancient Egyptians, Assyrians, Greeks, and Romans all used slaves. Early African empires also used slaves. The followers of many religions, including Jews, Christians, and Muslims, accepted slavery as natural. Before the 15th century, slaves were usually captives who had been taken in battle and afterward lived with their captors, sometimes almost as a part of the family. They often had most of the rights of other citizens, and their children could be born free. The chattel slavery of the Americas was very different. Africans were bought and sold, transported across the Atlantic, then sold again. Their children and their children's children were born as slaves.

The African slave trade that brought Harriet Tubman's grandparents to America began in 1444, when a fleet of Portuguese ships sailed into the African port of Lagos with 235 slaves aboard. The Portuguese, who had captured their prisoners in raids along the West African coast, sold them to an African king. After discovering how much money they could make selling captive Africans, other ship captains got involved. The Portuguese soon found that it was easier to buy slaves who had been captured by Africans than to carry on raids themselves. Within a few years, the Portuguese had an active slave-trading business in Europe and Africa. They bought and sold thousands of slaves a year. Nearly half a century before Columbus reached the New World, the Portuguese were trading cloth, brassware, glass beads, and oyster shells for slaves.

In the late 16th century, Europeans who settled in the West Indies and South America found a land of plenty. They soon discovered that they had more gold than they could dig and more rich soil than they could farm. The few Spanish and Portuguese settlers needed many people to work for them if they were to mine the gold and grow the crops that would make them rich. At first the Europeans tried to enslave the native tribes for manual labor. The Spaniards wanted the West Indian peoples to pan gold, and the Portuguese wanted the Brazilian tribes to raise sugar cane. But the original inhabitants of the New World were accustomed to having complete freedom, and they refused to work for the newcomers. Even those tribal people who could be forced to work became sick from diseases the white man had brought from Europe. One Spanish planter complained that the "[Indians] died like fish in a bucket."

The Spanish and the Portuguese soon came up with the same solution. They decided that West Africa could provide them with better slaves, people who were already experienced in many of the skills needed in the Americas. The West Africans had no written language, no wheel, and no plough, but they grew their own food, made metal tools, and seemed to possess great strength and endurance. Some Portuguese colonists thought that the Africans seemed perfect for the work. They thought God had made the people of Africa for the sole purpose of working in Portuguese-controlled Brazil. They believed that both the American land and the African people had been waiting for the Europeans to bring them together.

Spain soon joined Portugal in bringing African slaves to the West Indies and South America. At first the Spanish claimed they were importing the hardier Africans to spare the lives of the weak American natives. Soon it became obvious that Spain also enjoyed the wealth it gained from the slave trade.

After seeing how much money the Spanish and Portuguese were making by buying and selling slaves, the Dutch, the Danes, and the French got involved. In 1554, the British entered the slave trade. A little more than a century later, Great Britain had more slave ships than any other country. Most of its trade was in the West Indies, where the slaves were used to growing sugar cane. Much of the sugar cane was made into rum, which was then carried back to England in the same ships that had brought the slaves.

There were a few slaves in North America even before 1620, when the *Mayflower* landed at Plymouth. Twenty slaves from a Dutch slave ship arrived in Jamestown Colony in 1619, but it wasn't until tobacco became the most important crop in the colonies that North Americans began to import slaves regularly. Growing and curing tobacco in the huge quantities demanded by Europe required many hands. The monotonous, tiring work had to be done almost year-round.

The earliest North American slaves were treated much like indentured servants, people who agreed to serve a master for a given period of time. They were freed after they had served their time. In the American colonies, true indentured servants were western Europeans—mainly British. Most of them had agreed to become servants in order to get to the New World. Others signed contracts to escape prison or even death sentences. Still others had large debts they couldn't pay. And some were indentured through trickery. Most of these indentured servants were freed after five to seven years. Some of them, especially those who had previously been sentenced to death or long prison sentences, were forced to work most of their lives. Slaves, however, were not indentured servants. They had no contracts. Most importantly, they had all come to America against their will.

Because the demand for workers on the tobacco plantations was so great, the tobacco-growing colonies of Maryland and Virginia became major slave importers. Before long, plantation owners found it impractical to release their slaves. By 1640, some slaves were being held for their entire lives, and their children were born as slaves.

By the time the slave trade became important in North America, many decent men and women on both sides of the Atlantic had begun to speak out against it. Clergymen and others were appalled by the stories of greed and cruelty on the Middle Passage of slave ships. They wanted the trade stopped altogether. The Middle Passage was the second part of the slave ship's three-part voyage. First the ship left its home port, loaded with cloth, guns, salt, gunpowder, and glass beads for trade in Africa. On the Middle Passage, after trading its European cargo of goods for Africans, the ship sailed to a port in the West Indies or along the Atlantic coast of the Americas, where the slaves were sold. The ships then returned home, sometimes loaded with goods for sale in the home port. The people in the home port never actually saw the horror of the Middle Passage, where both the crews and their human cargo died in great numbers. The crews died of tropical diseases, such as malaria.

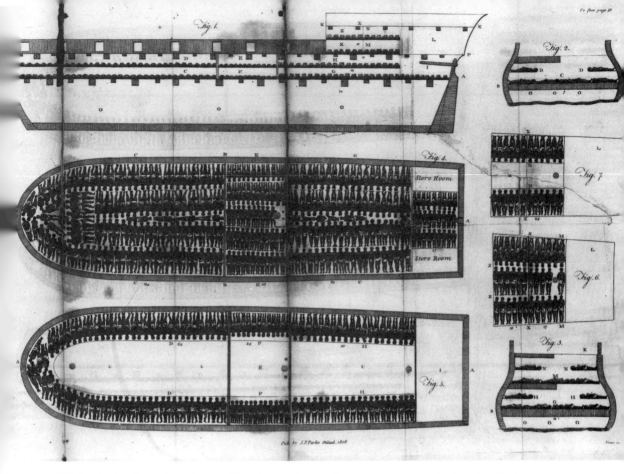

This deck plan of a slave ship shows how slaves were crowded onto shelves for weeks at a time.

They had built up no resistance to these diseases, and there was no known treatment for them. The slaves died of European diseases such as smallpox, diphtheria, and measles. Before 1754, when British ships began to carry limes on long voyages, both crew and slaves suffered from scurvy.

In the early days of the Atlantic trade, captains often packed the slaves so tightly together that they had to lie on their sides, crammed against one another for the entire journey.

The greedy companies gradually learned that this practice was costing them more money than it saved. It was better to arrive in port with healthy slaves who brought good prices than to lose part of their cargo on the way or to have to sell sick slaves. By 1684, all countries except Portugal had placed a limit on the number of slaves each ship could carry. Slaves were still chained together in leg irons, but ships were designed to allow more fresh air below. Slaves were even brought onto the deck sometimes.

By the 18th century, most captains of slavers, or slave ships, had begun to carry along a surgeon. They hoped to increase their profits by keeping the Africans in reasonably good health. On September 6, 1781, Luke Collingwood, captain of the *Zong,* loaded his ship on the African coast with a cargo of 400 slaves. By November 29, he had lost 7 crewmen and more than 60 slaves to an epidemic. Many more were sick. He discovered that he didn't have enough water to last the entire trip. He knew that if the slaves died from sickness or thirst, the shipowners would lose money. On the other hand, if the slaves died from drowning, the insurers would have to pay the owners for the loss. He chose 54 sick and weak slaves and threw them into the sea alive. Two days later, 42 more were thrown overboard. That same day it rained, and Collingwood collected 11 days' allowance of water in his casks. He wanted to make sure no more died aboard his ship, however, so he threw another 26 slaves overboard. Knowing they would be next, 10 more Africans jumped into the sea.

The slavers usually fed the captives two meals a day, but some slaves refused to eat the pulp of horse beans and lard they were given. Some starved to death. Others were force-fed. Some, unwilling to spend their lives as property, threw themselves overboard. In spite of all the hardships they endured, during the 400 years of trade, about 8 out of 10 Africans reached the New World alive. Although there are no accurate estimates of the number who died on their way from Africa to the New World, it is possible that as many as 100,000 died on their way to the colonies of North America alone.

Even though many people on both sides of the Atlantic opposed the slave trade, few people in America were against slavery itself. In the 17th and 18th centuries, slavery was practiced in all of the American colonies. Boston was one of the first American ports to get rich from the slave trade. Some of its most famous and respected families added to their fortunes by trading African slaves. Providence, Rhode Island, a shipbuilding town, was another northern city that profited from the trade. Prominent families of New York and

Philadelphia were involved. In fact, the American Revolution itself was partially financed with money from the slave trade.

Even so, slavery had its enemies in colonial America. The Quakers had fought against it from the beginning. Thomas Paine, who greatly influenced Thomas Jefferson, published an essay in 1775, "African Slavery in America," in which he said that slavery was no less immoral than "murder, robbery, lewdness and barbarity." In 1776, when Thomas Jefferson drafted the Declaration of Independence, he denounced the slave trade. In the first draft of the Declaration, Jefferson called the slave trade "a cruel war against human nature itself, violating its most sacred rights of life and liberty." Unfortunately, the Continental Congress removed the antislavery language because it displeased some Southerners and New Englanders. The final draft of the Declaration of Independence was a noble document that proclaimed the rights of everyone

This drawing shows the first slave sale on the North American continent.

to "Life, Liberty, and the pursuit of Happiness." But these fine words did not apply to the nearly 700,000 slaves whose labor helped build the new Republic.

Jefferson had a little more success with the Constitutional Convention of 1787. There Jefferson, James Madison, and Alexander Hamilton argued to outlaw slavery in the new Constitution. They did not get their way. The Constitution did, however, rule that after 20 years, Congress could make a federal law to prevent any more slaves from being imported from Africa. In 1807, Congress voted to end the slave trade. This law would be effective beginning January 1, 1808. Some historians estimate that another 33,000 slaves were illegally imported from Africa after Congress had officially put an end to the slave trade. In 1820, around the time Harriet Tubman was born, there were 1,538,022 slaves in America. When the Civil War began, the total slave population of the United States was nearly 4,000,000. The Atlantic slave trade was dead, but slavery itself lived on.

BORN INTO SLAVERY

"Children have their sorrows as well as men and
    women. . . . "

FREDERICK DOUGLASS
My Bondage and My Freedom

bout 40 years before the Civil War began, a slave child,
Araminta, was born on a plantation in Dorchester County
on Maryland's eastern shore. Bucktown was the closest
town. Baltimore was 60 miles north, on the western shore of the
Chesapeake Bay. The Mason-Dixon Line—which separated Maryland from Pennsylvania, the North from the South, and the free
states from the slave states—was 100 miles away. The year was
either 1820 or 1821. Like others born into slavery, Araminta, who
later became known as Harriet Ross Tubman, was never to know her
birth date. Her parents, Harriet Greene and Benjamin Ross, couldn't
read or write. They didn't even know the months of the year. They
simply kept track of life by the seasons: summer, winter, harvest time,
and planting time. They had no family records beyond their own
memories to document the births of their 11 children.

The most important fact about Harriet Tubman's birth was not
the date or the place, or even who her parents were. It was that she
was, from the day she was born, the property of Edward Brodas,
who owned her parents. A child was a slave if either her mother or
father was a slave.

Highlights in the Life of Harriet Tubman

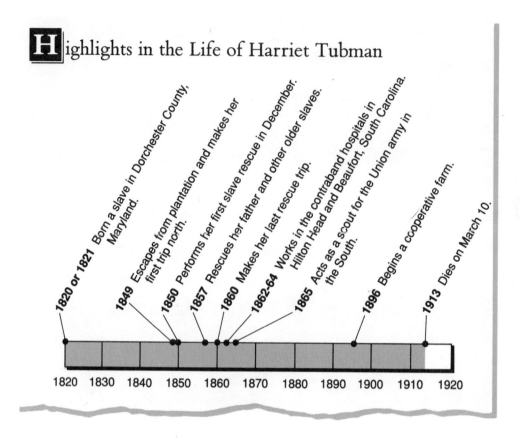

Brodas was probably disappointed that Rit, as Harriet Ross was called, had given birth to a daughter instead of a son. Male slaves were worth more than females, and times were hard in Maryland. In the years past, the Brodas plantation had grown tobacco, but tobacco soon wears out the soil. In 1820, most Maryland plantation owners were growing other crops, such as corn and wheat, in an effort to keep things going.

A plantation was more than a big farm. It was a little nation, with its own language, rules, and customs. Each plantation was not only self-sufficient, but cut off from the rest of the world. Even the language spoken by the slaves varied from one plantation to another, depending on the slaves' origins. Some of the older slaves who had been imported from Africa still spoke their native language. Those who had been born into slavery spoke a mixture of English and their old tribal languages.

Although there were state laws to protect slaves, owners did not always obey them. A slave owner could have his slaves lashed for the slightest offense, real or imagined. The overseer, who saw to it that the slaves did their work, often carried both a hickory switch and a cowhide whip ready to use on the slave who moved either too slowly or too quickly, or who overslept in the morning. Slaves could be shot for talking back or for trying to defend themselves. There was a saying in Maryland that it cost only a half cent to kill a slave and another half cent to bury one.

Araminta's master, Edward Brodas, wasn't an evil man. He went to church, where he was taught that slavery was a natural part of life and that God had made white people better than black people.

He was taught that because he was born with the privilege of being white and wealthy, it was his responsibility to provide for those entrusted to his care. He didn't feel sorry for his slaves as they worked all day in the hot sun, because he honestly believed that the Africans were better suited to such labor than he himself was. He believed that they had been created for just such tedious, backbreaking work. When he heard his slaves singing as they worked among the tobacco plants, he liked to think it was a sign that they were happy.

Brodas provided very well for his own family, who lived in a large house and enjoyed fine food that was prepared and served by polite slaves. He was probably kind to those slaves he came in contact with every day, and pleased to see that they were very good at their jobs. He probably paid far less attention to the ones who were out of his sight at the slave quarters. On the large plantations, there were two classes of slaves: those who worked in the house and those who worked in the fields. Those few who worked in the big house were taught specialized skills and appropriate manners. Among these were the cooks, maids, and butlers, all of whom received certain privileges. They wore better clothes and ate better food than the others did. Some even slept inside the big house, where they might be called to take care of a crying baby, or serve a late-night visitor. Most plantation slaves, however, were field hands. These slaves never set foot in the big house. They lived in

SLAVE CONDITIONS

Slavery existed in North America from 1619 until the Civil War. Though many Americans opposed this inhuman institution, the fact remains that for 240 years slavery was a fact of life. It was economically good for many of the country's white citizens, especially plantation owners in the South, but it meant a harsh existence for millions of people of African origin. Typically, the conditions in which most slaves lived were little better than those of animals. Often, a dozen or more people lived crammed together in one room. One writer described such a "home" on a plantation in New York state at the beginning of the 1880s. "It was a dismal chamber, its only lights consisting of a few panes of glass, through which the sun never shone. The space between the loose boards of the floor and the uneven earth below was often filled with mud and water. Inmates of both sexes and all ages slept on those damp boards, like horses, with a little straw and a blanket."

Slaves pick cotton on a plantation. Slave children worked as soon as they were able.

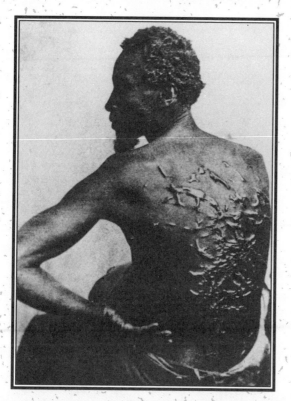

The scars on this man's back come from years of service as a slave.

Slave quarters offered little comfort and less shelter.

the slave quarters, a group of roughly built cabins that stood well out of sight of the big house.

Rit gave birth to Araminta in the dim light of one of these little cabins in the quarters. Its only room was dark because there were no windows and the rough walls were blackened by years of smoke from the large, open fireplace. The floor was made of clay. There was no furniture. No table, no chairs, no bedsteads. Minty, as Rit called her baby, was probably born on a folded blanket. Afterward Rit placed her daughter in a basket. When Minty outgrew the basket, she slept on the floor.

Araminta was fortunate, as a child, to have her mother near her. Some slave owners separated a mother from her children very soon after she stopped nursing. Sometimes the mother was sold or hired out to live and work on another farm. The marriages and families of slaves were not recognized by the law. It was up to the individual owners to acknowledge the families or not as they chose. Some thought no more of separating a slave mother from her young child than of separating a cow from its yearling calf. As a result, many slave children never knew their parents or their own brothers and sisters. Only during the later years of slavery did most owners try to keep families together.

After the invention of the cotton gin in 1793, it became possible for growers to process greater amounts of cotton than the average planter could produce. This created an even greater demand for slaves in the Deep South. Because bringing slaves from Africa had become illegal in 1808, slave owners in the Deep South—South Carolina, Georgia, Alabama, and Mississippi—had to import slaves from other states to work in their expanding cotton fields. Poor growing conditions in Maryland and a change in the demand for tobacco forced many plantation owners to free their extra slaves or sell them to slave traders.

When Araminta was still a little child, she saw two of her older sisters taken away by a trader. The young women were part of a coffle, or chain gang. She didn't know what would happen to her sisters. They might be put on a ship in Baltimore and taken down the coast, or they might be forced to walk overland, tied together in the ever-growing coffle. Many years later, Harriet still remembered the frightened, helpless look on her sisters' faces as they turned to look at their mother for the last time.

Another slave, Josiah Henson, who later escaped to Canada, remembered standing with his family on the auction block in Baltimore when he was a small boy. "My brothers and sisters were bid off one by one, while my mother, holding my hand, looked on in agony and grief," he said. His mother was separated from him and bought by a stranger. When she saw that little Josiah, her youngest child, was about to be sold to a different master, she pushed through the crowd and fell at the feet of her new owner, begging him to buy her little boy. Her master kicked her away as though she were a dog.

Araminta was allowed to stay with Rit at night. During the day, she and the other children who were too young to work were left in the care of one of the grandmothers, a woman who was no longer strong enough to work in the fields all day. Another slave remembered his early childhood as being a rather pleasant, carefree time. He said that nothing was expected of slave children. They didn't have to learn how to use a knife and fork because they had none. They didn't get scolded for being messy at the table because they ate on the same clay floor on which they slept. They were not spanked for tearing or soiling their clothes because they had practically no clothes. When they were bothered by the dirt on their skin, they bathed in the river, clothes and all. Slave children literally ran wild.

That brief freedom was the only good thing about the small child's life. There were few treats of any kind. The food was very simple. Even stingy owners were usually careful to feed the slaves adequately, because they wanted them to be healthy and strong enough to do the work. Brodas, Araminta's master, usually gave his field slaves an allotment of coarse cornmeal, with a small amount of smoked herring, and pork for the adults. Once a year he gave each family a baby pig to raise. Rit had no oven. She made unleavened cornmeal bread, much as the American Indians had, by baking a mixture of cornmeal and flour between two leaves that were placed in the embers. Ben and Rit took this "ashcake" into the fields with them as their main meal of the day.

A big black cooking pot hung by each family's fireplace. In this, the woman who cared for the smaller children made cornmeal mush for those too young to eat the gritty, ash-covered cakes. Sometimes the mush was eaten right from the pot. At other times it was poured into a long wooden trough, where the children scooped it up using clam or mussel shells for spoons.

In addition to the food allotment from the master, slaves could grow their own vegetables, go fishing or crabbing, and trap game. Of course, whatever the master wanted, he could take. Rit grew sweet potatoes, which she stored in a hole in the cabin floor, safe from bad weather and wild animals.

Once a year, the overseers handed out clothing to the slaves. Adult field hands received a pair of shoes and two changes of clothing for the year. The clothes were usually made of unbleached cotton muslin or tow linen, a rough cloth woven by the slaves. Older children, whether boys or girls, wore a long shirt with no trousers. Like other children who were too young to work in the fields, Araminta had no shoes. Sometimes slave children ran naked.

Along with the clothes, each adult man and woman received a blanket made of coarse, scratchy wool. The children usually had no blankets, but slept on straw pallets or the bare clay floor. In the cold damp of winter, they slept as close to the hearth as they could get, sometimes with their feet in the warm ashes.

Such as it was, Araminta's childhood came to an end when she was only six years old. Her hatred of slavery had just begun.

GOING TO WORK

"I was so little that I had to sit on the floor and
have the baby put in my lap. That baby was
always in my lap except when it was asleep or its
mother was feeding it."

HARRIET TUBMAN

Times were changing. On July 4, 1826, the 50th anniversary
of the Declaration of Independence, both Thomas Jefferson
and John Adams died. In 1827, New York State abolished, or
put an end to, slavery. Southerners were becoming uneasy.

When Araminta was a child, Maryland planters were no longer
growing much tobacco. They grew wheat and corn and hoped for
better times. The Brodas plantation wasn't as rich as it had once
been. The slaves knew this because many of them were disappear-
ing from the plantation. Some were sold. Others were hired out to
people who couldn't afford to buy their own slaves.

Little Minty wasn't sold because she was too young to be
"worth" much. To Edward Brodas, she was just another mouth to
feed. So he was pleased when a Mr. Cook, whose wife was a
weaver, took her from the plantation to work as an apprentice.
Apprentices were young helpers who learned a trade. Like indentured servants, they agreed to work for their master or mistress for
a certain number of years in exchange for the training. Araminta
was used to running free in the daytime and being near her mother
at night. At the Cooks' house, she was kept inside, where her

mistress made her sit still and do tiresome chores. At night she slept on the floor in a corner by the big black stove. The lint from the weaver's yarn made Araminta cough and sneeze. She wasn't at all interested in becoming a weaver and having to sit all day in a workhouse, so she paid little attention to her work.

Mrs. Cook soon gave up on Araminta, so Mr. Cook decided to try her at another job. He had her check his muskrat traps, which were set along the banks of a small stream. In order to see whether a trap had snared a muskrat, Araminta had to wade waist-deep into the cold water. Unfortunately, one day she didn't feel good; she had measles, and the cold water made her very sick. Rit took her home and nursed her back to health.

When Araminta was well, Mr. Cook took her back, and his wife again tried to teach her how to weave. Araminta still didn't want to learn, so she was returned to the Brodas plantation. The Cooks thought she couldn't be trained.

Shortly after this, a white woman came to the Brodas house looking for someone to take care of her child and do other chores. Because the woman couldn't afford to pay very much, Brodas didn't want to hire out one of his experienced slaves. He decided to try Araminta again. She was now a scrawny seven-year-old who didn't seem bright enough to follow the simplest instructions. Her master probably thought he was lucky to get anything at all for her. Araminta was put into the woman's wagon without a word of explanation and driven off.

After a while, the wagon stopped beside the woman's house. Araminta had never been inside her master's house or in any house other than the Cooks' and the cabins of the quarters. The woman's house wasn't very fine, but it seemed so to little Minty. It had a wooden floor and several rooms, including a parlor that was furnished with tables, chairs, and oil lamps. Araminta had never seen such nice things.

Apparently her new mistress, Miss Susan, had never had a servant before, because she seemed to have no understanding of her own responsibility toward the child. Without giving her instructions, Miss Susan told Araminta to sweep and dust the parlor. Because she had swept out the cabin many times, Araminta already knew how to sweep, but since her own home had no furniture, she had never dusted. After sweeping the floor, she dusted the mantel, tables, and chairs, but the dust stirred up by the broom settled on the furniture again, so that by the time the mistress came to see how her servant was doing, everything was dusty.

Miss Susan shrieked and scolded Araminta, instructing her to do the job over again. Again, the child did the best she could. She swept and dusted, just as she had before. In a few minutes, her mistress returned to inspect the parlor. Again she found her furniture covered with dust. This time Miss Susan whipped Araminta and told her to do the work over. The child tried again and again, but each time her best efforts resulted in another whipping by the angry woman. At some point, another woman appeared in the parlor. Miss Susan's sister, Emily, had heard Araminta's screaming and guessed what the problem was.

As Harriet Tubman remembered the incident many years later, Miss Emily asked, "Why do you whip the child, Susan, for not doing what she has never been taught to do? Leave her to me a few minutes, and you will see that she will soon learn how to sweep and dust a room." Miss Emily explained to Araminta that the dust came back because it was still hanging in the air from the sweeping. She opened the windows and told Araminta to sweep the floor, then leave the room until the dust had settled. Miss Emily said she should have no trouble dusting the furniture after that. Araminta did as she was told, and the room finally passed Miss Susan's inspection.

But the little girl's troubles weren't over. Her most important duty was caring for Miss Susan's baby. Many years later Harriet said, "I was so little that I had to sit on the floor and have the baby put in my lap. That baby was always in my lap except when it was asleep or its mother was feeding it." Araminta tended the baby all day, and at night she was expected to keep it from crying by rocking its cradle while Miss Susan slept. Whenever the baby's crying awakened its mother, she would lash Araminta with the cowhide whip she kept beside her bed. The whip did more than sting; it left scars on the child's neck and back. Sixty years later, those scars were still visible.

Miss Susan fed Araminta table scraps, but there were so few of them that she was always hungry. Hunger once got her into the worst trouble she had ever known. She had been standing near a sugar bowl while Miss Susan and her husband quarreled. She later told a friend: "Now you know, I never had anything good, no sweet, no sugar; and that sugar, right by me, did look so nice, and my mistress's back was turned to me while she was fighting with her husband, so I just put my fingers in the sugar bowl to take one lump and maybe she heard me for she turned and saw me. The next minute she had the rawhide down. I give one jump out of the door and I saw that they came after me, but I just flew and they didn't catch me. I ran and I ran and I passed many a house, but I didn't dare to stop, for they all knew my mistress and they would send me back."

There was no place to go. Araminta didn't know her way back to the Brodas farm. She hid for several days in a pigsty, trying to grab a few potato peels before the old sow chased her off. Half-starved, she eventually had to go back to Miss Susan and her whip.

Shortly after this incident, Araminta was returned to Brodas. By this time the child was sick and scarred from the whippings and worn down by lack of food and sleep. Araminta, who had grieved for her mother and the lost freedom of childhood, seemed sullen to her mistress. Miss Susan told Brodas, "She wasn't worth six-pence." The little girl returned to the quarters. Once again, Rit nursed her back to health.

As soon as Araminta was strong again, her master hired her out. It was clear to him that she would never be a good house servant. He decided she would probably be better off in the fields and hired her out to a man who wanted her for odd jobs. She was still very small, but her new master expected her to do heavy work. He made her chop wood and load it onto his wagon. If she was unable to lift a heavy load, he whipped her.

Araminta labored in his field, doing the work of an adult. She had still never worn a pair of shoes, but she had outgrown the tow-linen shirt of childhood and now wore a long dress. When she was 11 years old, as was the custom among slaves, she started wearing a bright cotton bandanna wound around her head to indicate that she was no longer a child. She was no longer known by her "basket name." Now she would be called Harriet.

In 1831, a disturbing story reached the white households. Even though they tried to keep it from the slaves, the story soon spread through the slave quarters like wildfire. On August 21, in Southampton County, Virginia, a slave known as Nat Turner had led an insurrection, or bloody rebellion, in which 55 white people, including women and children, were killed in their homes. The news horrified white Southerners and heartened their slaves.

Nat Turner was born the property of Benjamin Turner, who said the small child had "too much sense" to be raised as a slave. Benjamin Turner predicted that if Nat did remain a slave, he wouldn't be a very good one. Nat's own grandmother told him that he had been chosen by God for great work. Nat quickly learned to read and write. Because the people around him—both black and white—considered him to be especially gifted, Nat felt a responsibility to live up to his reputation. Nat became a lay preacher and began to believe that God had chosen him to free his people. He began to have visions and hear voices. Guided by these voices, the Prophet, as African Americans called Turner, developed a plan. He would lead an insurrection.

In 1830, Nat Turner was bought by Joseph Travis. Of Travis, Nat later said, he "was to me a kind master, and placed the greatest confidence in me." The Prophet waited for a sign from God that the time was right to start "the great work." Just after midnight on August 21, 1831, after receiving a "sign," Turner and four other slaves started the rebellion by killing five members of the sleeping Travis family.

During the next two days, Turner and his followers went to house after house, killing white occupants and seizing their weapons and other valuables. At each place, the Prophet recruited, or gathered, slaves for his insurrection. Turner planned to get more

This drawing depicts the capture of Nat Turner, who led a bloody rebellion of escaped slaves.

weapons by capturing the armory in Jerusalem, Virginia. The rebels would steal the weapons at the armory and then hide out in the Dismal Swamp, from which they would be able to carry on their war indefinitely.

But nothing worked as planned. Turner and a party of 20 slaves started for Jerusalem, but he soon realized that his recruits were deserting and he wouldn't have enough men to take the armory. He turned back. Turner had expected hundreds of slaves to join the insurrection, but there were fewer than 75. Nat Turner had followers, because he was persuasive, but he was neither a strategist nor a leader. He had no skill in planning and carrying out a rebellion, and his little army had no discipline. Within two months of their rampage, he and many of his followers were captured. They were tried, convicted, and 17 of his recruits were hanged. Turner gave a long, detailed confession to Dr. Thomas R. Gray, a physician who visited him in prison. Turner was tried on November 5 and executed on November 11, 1831.

Nat Turner's rebellion frightened white Southerners so much that the states quickly passed a series of oppressive laws. Because Turner could read and write, new statutes made it a crime to educate a slave. Because he had recruited other slaves to his cause, new laws made it a crime for slaves to assemble. This meant that they couldn't have church services or talk to each other in the fields. They were even forbidden to sing certain spirituals, such as "Go Down Moses," because whites believed that such words as "set my people free" were signals for rebellion or escape. In addition, proslavery forces viewed the white abolitionists in the South as traitors. They were arrested for the flimsiest reasons.

Southerners—both black and white—knew that the issue of slavery was a powder keg just waiting for a spark.

WILLIAM LLOYD GARRISON

"I will be as harsh as truth and as
uncompromising as justice. . . . I will not
equivocate—I will not excuse—I will not retreat
a single inch—and I will be heard."

WILLIAM LLOYD GARRISON
Liberator, January 1, 1831

arriet Tubman knew about Nat Turner, and she knew about people in Dorchester County who helped slaves escape, but she had no idea how many people were fighting to destroy slavery. On April 7, 1830, nearly a year and a half before the Prophet's rebellion, a young white man was locked up in Baltimore City Jail. He would remain there for 49 days.

At that time, Baltimore was one of the major centers of the domestic slave trade—slave trade among the states. The man, William Lloyd Garrison, was an abolitionist—an outspoken enemy of slavery. Because he believed it was both immoral and unlawful, he wanted slavery abolished immediately. Four months earlier, in January 1830, Garrison had read an announcement that the *Francis,* a ship owned by Francis Todd of Newburyport, Massachusetts, was sailing for New Orleans with a cargo of slaves. He had written an article for the abolitionist paper, *Genius of Universal Emancipation,* accusing Todd and the ship's captain of being "highway robbers and murderers." He said the two men should be "sentenced to solitary confinement for life." Francis Todd accused Garrison of libel—that is, of writing damaging things about him that were untrue. The state of Maryland found Garrison guilty and fined him $50, which he refused to pay. He refused because he hoped his imprisonment would call attention to the thriving slave trade along the Atlantic coast.

Garrison was born in 1805. When he was three years old, the embargo against importing slaves put many people in New England out of work. His father was one of those people. As a little boy, Garrison had to go from door to door begging for food. At the age of 12, he became an apprentice at the Newburyport *Herald*. The boy learned quickly, and learned much more than the trade of printing. By reading the stories he set in type, he got an education in current affairs and politics. He was particularly interested in the struggles of the world's oppressed people.

Garrison finished his apprenticeship in 1825. By 1826, he was publishing his own paper, the *Free Press,* in Newburyport. His

paper was full of political articles supporting the need for the states to stand together. The paper didn't do very well. Within a year, he gave up and moved to Boston, where he felt he had a better chance of succeeding. For a time he worked for the *National Philanthropist,* an abolitionist paper.

Garrison was a very religious man, a born reformer who campaigned against anything he considered to be immoral. In 1828, he found the cause to which he would devote the rest of his life. In March of that year, he met the Quaker Benjamin Lundy, an antislavery reformer. Lundy had traveled all over the country, speaking against slavery and founding antislavery groups. He and other Quakers believed that the way to fight slavery was to boycott—that is, refuse to buy—anything that had been produced by slave labor, such as sugar, cotton, and tobacco. Other people who opposed slavery thought it could be ended by requiring owners to pay wages to their slaves. This would eventually allow slaves to buy their freedom. Still others thought it was the responsibility of the federal government to buy the slaves' freedom.

The most popular early antislavery movement started in 1821, at about the time Harriet Tubman was born. It was called the American Colonization Society, and its members bought part of the country now called Liberia as a home for the slaves. Henry Clay, Daniel Webster, and James Madison were among the society's members. The society collected large amounts of money to purchase slaves from their masters and ship them to the new colony.

Many colonizationists, or supporters of the society, had reasons other than mere goodwill. Northerners worried about the growing number of freed and escaped slaves who were crossing the Mason-Dixon Line, the border between free and slave states. These Northerners thought there were already too few jobs. To colonizationists, however, the idea of sending the slaves "home" to Africa seemed to be a humane and reasonable solution to this very serious problem.

When Garrison first heard Lundy speak in 1828, the Quaker said the slaves should be sent to Liberia only if they wanted to go. Garrison had always believed that slavery was wrong. But he had never heard anyone present a real plan for abolishing it. He was

Publisher William Lloyd Garrison, who sought ways to bring an end to slavery in the United States.

immediately converted to Lundy's way of thinking. In order to have a means of expressing his thoughts on the issue of slavery, Garrison agreed to publish a political journal in Bennington, Vermont. The paper was called the *Journal of Our Times,* and he published it for a year before its readership fell off.

In Baltimore, meanwhile, Benjamin Lundy also published a paper—the *Genius of Universal Emancipation*. He had read Garrison's *Journal* and liked the strong, clear way in which the young man spoke out against slavery. Lundy decided it would be good to have someone like Garrison to help him edit the *Genius* and to run the paper while he was away on speaking tours. Garrison was glad to accept Lundy's offer. When his contract with the paper in Bennington ended, he headed for Baltimore. On his way, he stopped in Boston, where he met another abolitionist, William Goodell. Before talking with Goodell, Garrison had agreed with Lundy's views about gradual emancipation (freeing of the slaves) and the usefulness of colonization. Now Goodell convinced him that the slaves should be freed at once, and that sending the former slaves to Africa would be wrong.

When Garrison arrived in Baltimore, Lundy was surprised by his changed outlook. He didn't agree with Garrison, but he was willing to work with the young man. Lundy changed his mind, however, when Garrison was found guilty of libel in the Todd case. He was afraid the anger Garrison stirred up in slaveholders would hurt the cause of abolition. He ended the partnership.

Garrison had to serve a jail sentence when he refused to pay the fine for libel. As soon as he was released, he left Baltimore. He wanted to start a new journal, which he intended to call the *Public Liberator and Journal of the Times.* The journal was to be devoted to "the abolition of slavery and the moral and intellectual elevation of our colored population." He needed support for his new enterprise, so he went to several cities to speak in favor of immediate emancipation. He appealed to abolitionists in Philadelphia, New York, and Boston, but had no luck. They all believed that gradual emancipation, with colonization, was the best way to end slavery.

Finally, Garrison went to Abner Kneeland, who was head of the Society for Free Enquirers. Kneeland and his followers allowed Garrison to use their hall for his lectures, which drew large audiences of abolitionists, including some of the most famous people of the time.

Garrison was a good, plain speaker. He soon had the public support he needed to start his paper, but he still needed money, a press, and a place in which to work. He persuaded an old friend from the *Philanthropist,* Isaac Knapp, to become his partner. On January 1, 1831, Knapp and Garrison published the first issue of the *Public Liberator and Journal of the Times.*

The *Liberator,* as the journal became known, wasn't an immediate success. Garrison and Knapp had to struggle to keep it going. They worked 14 hours a day and slept where they worked. Arthur Tappan, a wealthy and powerful abolitionist, sent them money

The masthead of *The Liberator*, William Lloyd Garrison's antislavery newspaper.

from New York, but most of their subscribers were freed slaves who lived in Boston, Philadelphia, and New York.

Freed and escaped slaves who came to the northern cities were often saddened to learn that they weren't considered full-fledged citizens. Black children were allowed to get an education, but the schools were segregated—that is, whites and blacks went to separate schools. The same white churches that favored abolition and raised money for colonization often excluded black people from membership. Garrison, with his direct language and strong stand against colonization, became very popular among African Americans.

Even though the *Liberator* had no subscribers in the South, Garrison was much quoted there. A North Carolina paper accused him of inciting, or helping to start, Nat Turner's rebellion through his writings. Other papers throughout the South made similar accusations. That same year, someone offered a $5,000 reward for Garrison's arrest and conviction "under the laws of Georgia." Plainspoken and abrasive though he was, Garrison was a pacifist. He opposed all war and violence. He called Turner's actions "phrenzied, anti-Christian," and said they had hurt the cause of abolition.

Not all of Garrison's enemies were in the South. As time went on, and colonization lost favor, many Northerners saw Garrison as a troublemaker. In Boston, on October 21, 1835, the mayor had to rescue Garrison from a mob of well-dressed men who wanted to hang him. He was put into jail for his own safety. On the cell wall he wrote:

William Lloyd Garrison was put into this cell on Monday afternoon, October 21, 1835, to save him from the violence of a respectable and influential mob, who sought to destroy him for preaching the abominable [terrible] and dangerous doctrine that all men are created equal, and that all oppression is odious [disgusting] in the sight of God.

5

FIELD HAND

"They said I wasn't worth a penny."

HARRIET TUBMAN

While William Lloyd Garrison fought a war of words for immediate emancipation, Harriet Tubman continued to live and work as a slave. Because she was unable to read, her only contact with the world outside of the plantation was by word of mouth. Harriet had heard of the Prophet and his uprising. She had heard of his hanging. She also knew that there were some white people right in Dorchester County who helped runaway slaves. They were called Quakers. She knew, too, that by following the North Star far enough, she could reach freedom. She had not yet heard of the plainspoken man in Boston and his battle on her behalf.

Sometimes Harriet thought about running away, but she didn't know how to go about it, or how to reach the people who could help her. So she did her work as well as she could, day by day. She liked being outside. The harder she worked, the stronger she became. People who knew her later said that in spite of her small size, she was as strong as a man. She could lift heavy loads and work long hours at any job she was given.

Unfortunately, when Harriet was in her early teens, she received an injury that would affect her for the rest of her life. She had been hired out to a farmer named Barrett. It was harvesttime. The slaves were working in the evening, cleaning wheat and husking corn. Harriet saw one of them leave his work. She watched as he crossed a nearby field, heading for the village store. Suspecting that he was running away, she followed him.

The overseer had noticed him, too. The runaway was young and strong, very valuable to his master. The overseer chased him on foot until the man, followed by Harriet, ran into the store, where he was cornered. The overseer wanted the slave whipped as an example for the rest of the slaves. He asked Harriet and others to help tie him up. When she refused, the overseer grabbed a two-pound weight from a feed scale and threw it as hard as he could at the runaway. The weight missed him and hit Harriet in the middle of her forehead. She fell to the floor unconscious, her scalp bleeding profusely and her forehead half caved in by the blow.

She was carried back to the slave quarters, where the other slaves kept a vigil. No one expected her to live through the night. Rit prayed for her and tended to her wound all through that night and for many days and nights to come. After a time, Harriet regained consciousness. The wound healed, but it left a depression in her forehead and a scar that disfigured her for life.

Harriet was eventually able to get up from her straw pallet on the floor, but the injury left her with severe headaches and seizures that caused her to fall asleep without warning in the middle of whatever she was doing. She might be working or talking when one of the seizures hit her. Sometimes she even fell asleep in the middle of a sentence. When she awoke minutes later, she would finish it as though nothing had happened. Harriet never recovered from this strange affliction.

Many years after the incident, Harriet remembered that her master had brought men to look at her while she was still sick, hoping to sell her. He knew it would be some time before he would be able to hire her out again. As she remembered it, he tried to sell her for the lowest possible price. No one wanted her. "They said I wasn't worth a penny," she said many years later.

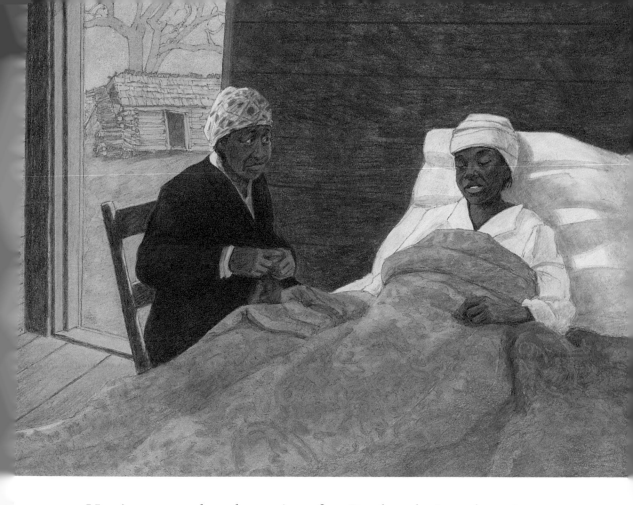

Harriet remembered praying for Brodas during that time,
hoping he would have a change of heart and become a better man.
But when she heard that her master planned to sell her to a chain
gang, Harriet changed her prayer. She prayed, "Lord, if you ain't
never going to change that man's heart, *kill him,* Lord, and take
him out of the way, so he won't do no more mischief."

Shortly after that, Harriet learned that Brodas had died. She
blamed herself for his death. She remembered feeling so guilty that
she prayed all the time. "I was always talking to the Lord. When I
went to the horse trough to wash my face, and took up the water in
my hands, I said, 'Oh, Lord, wash me, make me clean.' When I
took up the towel to wipe my face and hands, I cried, 'Oh, Lord,
wipe away all my sins!'"

Harriet had good reason to worry. Whenever a slave owner died,
the slaves he owned were disposed of like any other property. If he
left a will, he might set them free, give them to his heirs, or have

them sold to a slave trader. But if he died without leaving a will, the slaves were divided among his heirs. The new owners could do whatever they wished with them. Brodas left his slaves to his son. The son was still a child, so Brodas's will appointed Dr. Anthony Thompson, a preacher from Bucktown, to run the plantation.

The slave families on the Brodas plantation were afraid they would be separated, sold, and scattered all over Maryland. All sorts of rumors spread in the slave quarters. The slaves' greatest fear was that they would be sold to the traders. Fortunately, Brodas had left instructions to Thompson telling him not to sell his slaves outside of the state. Still, the slaves were uneasy. They feared the chain gangs of the traders, the heartlessness of the auction block, and the separation from their families. They had heard terrible rumors of how slaves were treated in the huge cotton and sugarcane fields of the Deep South. Many of these rumors were probably very true, no matter how ugly they seemed to be.

Frederick Law Olmsted, a writer and a famous landscape architect, had heard many stories of slavery in the Deep South that he thought must be exaggerated. He believed differently when he visited a plantation in Georgia. There he saw a group of nearly 200 slaves moving across the fields in parallel lines. Behind them, a big surly driver cracked his whip, shouting, "Shove your hoe, there! Shove your hoe!" The slaves worked like this from before sunrise until after sunset. Their only time off was for their noonday meal.

Olmsted later said to one of the overseers, "It must be very disagreeable to punish them as much as you do." The overseer said, "Yes, it would be to those of you who are not used to it—but it's my business, and I think nothing of it. Why, sir, I wouldn't mind killing a nigger more than I would a dog." Olmsted asked him if he had ever killed a black person. He said, "Not quite." He said that sometimes killing became necessary because some blacks were determined not to let a white man whip them.

Shortly after that, as Olmsted was riding with the overseer, they discovered a young slave woman hiding in the brush. She had slipped away from the others to avoid work. The overseer whipped her until she was raw and bleeding. When Olmsted asked why it was necessary to whip her so severely, the overseer answered, "If I hadn't punished her so hard, she would have done the same thing again tomorrow, and half the people on the plantation would have followed her example."

In 1861, Olmsted would write a book, *Journeys and Explorations in the Cotton Kingdom,* that gave a shocking picture of slavery. But many slave owners and others who defended slavery probably pointed out that only the worst cases were made public. They would say that most slave owners, especially on the smaller plantations, cared about their slaves. Most slave owners weren't rich men. The 1830 U.S. Census showed that a quarter of the white people in Maryland owned slaves. One Maryland man owned 300, but most slave owners had only 5 or 6. On the smaller farms, owners knew their slaves as individuals, and many of them hated to break up the slave families. In fact, many intelligent owners knew that the slaves were less likely to run away when their families were kept together. Even when forced by hard times or a death to sell their slaves, some owners would sell them only as families. Sales records from Richmond and Alexandria show that women were usually sold with their youngest children, and husbands and wives were often sold together.

No matter how kind a master was, however, he could not change the basic reality of slavery—the fact that one person could be born free and another could be born property. Harriet Tubman knew little about law, but she knew that a system that gave one person the right to own another was evil. When she was a child, she had run from Miss Susan's whip. As a woman, she awaited her chance to run away again—not from Dr. Thompson, her new master, but from slavery itself.

MARRIAGE

"I had reasoned this out in my mind; there was one of two things I had a *right* to, liberty or death; if I could not have one, I would have the other. ...."

HARRIET TUBMAN

After Edward Brodas died, Harriet worked in the house of John Stewart. He was more lenient than many of her previous masters. Harriet's father, Ben Ross, had been hired out to Stewart to supervise the cutting and hauling of timber for use in the Baltimore shipyards. Ben was very good at what he did, and he often earned as much as $5 a day. Harriet got permission from her master to "hire her time." This meant that for about $75 a year, Harriet could buy the right to find work on her own. She had to give the master part of her earnings, but she could keep what was left for herself. She found jobs driving oxen, carting, and plowing. One year she made enough money for herself to buy a pair of oxen worth $40.

Sometimes Harriet worked for her father cutting wood and hauling logs. She didn't make as much money as he did because she couldn't do as much work, but she could still cut, chop, and stack half a cord (about 64 cubic feet) of firewood in a day.

In 1844, when she was about 23 years old, Harriet married John Tubman. Usually slaves had little choice in marriage. Their masters decided for them. Because of Harriet's sleeping spells, her master probably thought she wouldn't make a good mother, so he didn't try to marry her off as a young girl. In later life, Harriet rarely talked about her marriage to John Tubman. There is evidence that she loved him very much, but they weren't very happy together.

Papers such as this one were the only proof of freedom for a former slave.

John Tubman was one of more than 62,000 freed slaves in Maryland at that time. Such a large number of free blacks worried many white people. They saw the increasing number of freedmen and freedwomen as a threat to the whole society. There were three times as many free African Americans in Maryland as there were in New York State. In Delaware, free African Americans greatly outnumbered slaves. Some white Marylanders wanted to get rid of all the free blacks. Taking a cue from the colonization movement in the North, the Maryland Colonization Society had started its own colony in Liberia. Unlike such abolitionists as Benjamin Lundy, who wanted to free the slaves and send them to Liberia, the Maryland colonizationists wanted to keep all of their 90,000 slaves "in their place." The southern colonizationists wanted to send only those African Americans who were already free to Liberia, whether or not they wanted to go.

Being a free African American in Maryland was only a little better than being a slave. John Tubman had a few basic rights, though. He had the right to travel from place to place. He could own property and "improve his condition." This means he could earn and save money without having to pay a master. But he had to compete with hired-out slaves for whatever work there was, and many African-American people had been freed in the first place because there wasn't enough work for them as slaves. This meant that a free African American like John either had to have exceptional skills or had to accept work for a lower daily rate than the slaves who were hiring out.

John also had his own cabin, but he didn't live much better than the people in the slave quarters. In some ways, he might even have been worse off. Sanitation was very poor for everyone during these times. Plumbing was rare, and there were no sewers to carry off waste. It was hard to find a source of water that was safe to drink. A good well had to be dug by hand, usually by many slave hands. Poor people like John had to rely on cisterns—barrels or holes dug in the ground for catching rainwater. After a flood, when epidemics of typhoid fever and cholera swept through the land and polluted water supplies, free African Americans were in greater

danger than most slaves. Records show that these epidemics
sickened and killed many more free blacks than either whites or
slaves. Those very records convinced slaveholders that African-
American people needed the "protection" of slavery.

John Tubman didn't think so. He valued his freedom more than
anything else. He knew that once he had been freed, his master
couldn't enslave him again. But he also knew that the farther he
wandered from home, the less safe he would become. The piece of
paper he carried identifying himself as a freedman couldn't protect
him from the evil men who preyed on African Americans. John
had heard rumors of white kidnappers who didn't care that a black
man had been emancipated. They cared only that he be healthy
enough to bring a good price in the Deep South.

Solomon Northrup's story is an example of the dangers free
African Americans like John faced. Northrup, who had lived in
New York all his life, was the educated son of freed slaves. He was a
hardworking, successful young businessman and a talented musi-
cian. In 1841, while he was in Washington, D.C., young Northrup
was drugged, kidnapped, and taken to Louisiana. There he was
sold to Edwin Epps. Even though Northrup had papers to prove
that he was a free man, he was forced to work as Epps's slave for 12
years. He was released only when the governor of New York
finally succeeded in freeing him.

When Northrup returned to his home, he wrote a book about
his experiences as a slave. In the book, he described Epps as a man
"who has never enjoyed the advantages of an education." Epps
drank heavily, and when he was drunk he enjoyed "lashing [his
slaves] about the yard with his long whip, just for the pleasure of
hearing them screech and scream, as the great welts were planted
on their backs." In the cotton fields, Epps, a former overseer, rode
behind the slaves on horseback. As they hoed, he whipped those
who either lagged behind the rest or passed the leader. During the
hoeing season, Northrup wrote, "the lash is flying from morning
until night, the whole day long."

The picking season brought a new form of torture. Northrup
wrote that few sights were more beautiful than a cotton field in

bloom, pure and white as far as the eye could see. Unfortunately, for the slave the view was spoiled by having to pick at least 200 pounds of cotton a day. At the end of the day, each slave's cotton was weighed. Slaves who didn't pick as much as Epps thought they could received a lashing for their day's pay. One woman with very quick hands could pick 500 pounds on her best days, so she was whipped whenever she picked less than that, even though she was picking twice as much as most of the other slaves.

Because free African Americans like John Tubman were always in danger of losing their freedom and ending up picking cotton in the Deep South, it's no wonder that he didn't want to leave his home. Perhaps he also suspected that the North wasn't the heaven Harriet thought it was. Over and over, she told John of a dream she'd kept having at night: "I seemed to see a line, and on the other side of the line were green fields, and lovely flowers, and beautiful white ladies, who stretched out their arms to me over the line, but I couldn't reach them. I always fell before I got to the line."

John didn't believe in Harriet's dream. He didn't want to leave his homeland and the people he had known all his life for an unknown and perhaps dangerous world. Also, to go north Harriet would have to run away. John so disliked hearing Harriet talk about running away that he threatened to report her to her master.

Harriet, too, wondered if there might not be an easier way to freedom. She asked John how he had become free. He explained that his family had been freed because a former master, who had no children, died without leaving a will. Something she had heard Rit say about her past stuck in Harriet's mind. She took $5 from her savings and paid a lawyer to search the records of Dorchester County. She found that Rit had been left to a woman named Mary Patterson, who had died young. Patterson had left no will, and she had no heirs. Her death had legally freed Rit from bondage, but Rit remained a slave because no one ever told her she was free. As a result, all of her children were born as slaves.

Harriet, growing more and more unhappy with her state, continued to hire herself out. After a few years of living with her husband in his cabin, she hired herself out to young Dr. Thompson and went to live on his plantation. Thompson was the son of her owner's guardian, and had befriended her in the past. Harriet worked for Thompson for two years, still doing outside work. Like many other slaves, she preferred to work in the fields, even though it meant having fewer privileges. At least there she wouldn't have to smile all the time and curtsy and pretend she loved being

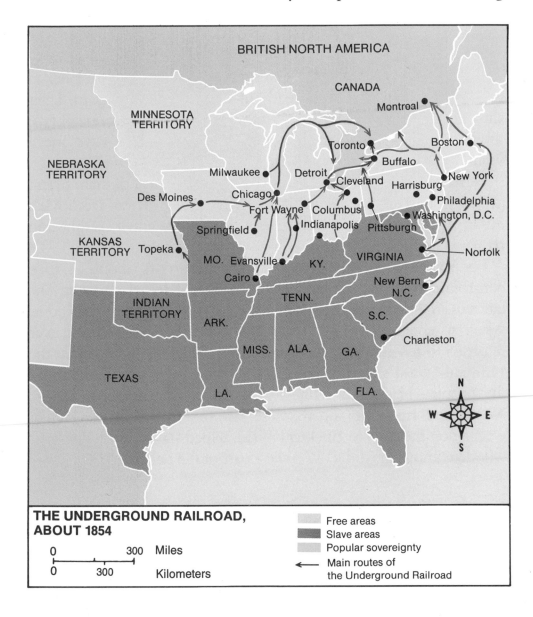

THE UNDERGROUND RAILROAD, ABOUT 1854

0 — 300 Miles
0 — 300 Kilometers

Free areas
Slave areas
Popular sovereignty
← Main routes of the Underground Railroad

owned and ordered about. And even though Harriet had to work very hard and long as a field hand, she could always return to her own people after work—and that was the closest thing she knew to freedom.

In 1849 young Brodas, Harriet's owner, died. This time the terrible rumor that spread through the slave quarters proved to be true. All of the slaves had to be sold. Harriet made up her mind that she wasn't going to be sold like a farm animal. She knew that few people in Dorchester County could afford to buy slaves, so she would probably be sold to a trader who would take her south to a cotton or cane plantation. She knew the time had come for her to run away, not just down the road but all the way to freedom. Later she said, "I had reasoned this out in my mind; there was one of two things I had a *right* to, liberty, or death; if I could not have one, I would have the other; for no man should take me alive."

Harriet knew that many slaves ran away, but most of them didn't get very far. They hid out just as she had when she ran from Miss Susan long ago. Within a few days, they were either caught and returned or they fell into the hands of slave catchers.

For many years now, there had been rumors about an Underground Railroad. When Harriet had first heard about it, she envisioned a long tunnel to freedom. She wondered how to find it, where to enter. It was as mysterious as death itself. No one ever returned to tell about it. As time went on, Harriet learned that the "railroad" wasn't a real train on a track but a way of talking about the people—black and white—who helped slaves escape to the North and freedom. There were rumors that a certain white woman on the road to Bucktown had helped slaves escape. Harriet wondered how she did it. Was she a part of the railroad to freedom?

FREDERICK DOUGLASS

"...we are *American citizens,* born with natural,
inherent, and just rights; [and the] scheme of the
American Colonization Society shall
never...drive *us* from our native soil."

FREDERICK DOUGLASS

W hile Harriet Tubman dreamed of freedom and waited for her chance to follow the North Star, many African-American people in the North were working to abolish slavery in other ways. In the 1840s, the black abolitionists were almost as divided as the whites on the best way to end slavery. Almost all blacks disagreed with those abolitionists who favored either gradual change or sending the slaves to Liberia. Most African-American abolitionists agreed with Garrison on the issue of colonization; they saw it as antiblack instead of antislavery. A growing number of African-American abolitionists admired Nat Turner's solution because black people had grown tired of words and thought that white slave owners needed more direct action. Some, influenced by Garrison, thought the United States Constitution itself was proslavery. They believed the country needed a new constitution that would better reflect the ideal expressed in the Declaration of Independence "that all men are created equal."

Some Northerners wanted to secede from the Union, to form a separate country, rather than be a part of slavery. But the goal of most abolitionists, whether black or white, was not to destroy the

Frederick Douglass, author, journalist, and escaped slave, spoke to whites about slavery.

country either by seceding or rebelling but by changing public opinion. Wendell Phillips, one of the leaders of the American Anti-Slavery Society, summed up the problem for abolitionists. He said that if the country were one big market, abolitionists would only have to show that slavery wasn't good business. If it were just a church, they would only have to show that slavery was immoral. If the nation were a college, abolitionists would only need logic and facts. "But," said Phillips, "we happen to live in the world—the world made up of thought and impulse, of self-conceit and self-interest, of weak men and wicked. To conquer, we must reach all."

If words alone had been enough, Frederick Douglass might have changed public opinion all by himself. Douglass, who had escaped from slavery in 1838, was becoming one of the most forceful voices raised against slavery. Douglass was a lecturer and journalist whose paper, *The North Star,* became an important force for African-American abolitionists. At first, because Douglass was so articulate and because his story was so unlikely, many people didn't believe he was really an escaped slave. He wrote: "They said I did not talk like a slave, look like a slave, nor act like a slave, and that they believed I had never been south of Mason and Dixon's line." To quiet his critics, he wrote *Narrative of the Life of Frederick Douglass, an American Slave* in 1845. Although the book silenced many of his critics, it also put Douglass in danger of being returned to his master.

To avoid being captured, Douglass sailed with Garrison and other abolitionists for Britain, where abolitionist speakers were very popular. Great Britain had abolished slavery 12 years earlier, in 1833. Without being asked, British audiences raised enough money to buy Douglass's freedom. As a result of Douglass's lectures and those of others—Charles Lenox Remond, William Powell, and William Wells Brown—people throughout Britain also sent valuables to be sold at Boston's antislavery bazaar, a major source of funding for the abolitionist movement in the United States.

Frederick Douglass was born in 1817 on a plantation in Talbot County, on the eastern shore of Maryland. This was three or four years before Harriet Tubman was born. His mother, Harriet Bailey, was a slave who was said to have remarkable intelligence. She named her son Frederick Augustus Washington Bailey. Douglass never knew who his father was, but some of the old slaves whispered that his master was his father.

Douglass's life as a slave was very different from Tubman's. He was separated from his mother and raised by his grandmother, Betsy Bailey. Frederick ran free until he was seven, when his grandmother took him to the home of his master, Captain Aaron Anthony. Anthony lived in a large house on another of the three farms that he owned. He also managed from 20 to 30 farms and several hundred slaves for Colonel Edward Lloyd. While Frederick worked for Anthony, he did typical farm-boy chores. He brought in cows from the pasture to the barn, kept chickens out of the garden, and swept the front yard.

At Captain Anthony's, Frederick saw how cruel and indifferent his master could be. Once he saw one of his own cousins beg for the master's protection from a drunken overseer who had lashed her with a cowhide whip. Her head and shoulders were covered with blood, but the master ordered her to go back to the overseer. He said she "deserved every bit of it." During his time at Anthony's, Frederick also learned how much better life was for the master than it was for the slaves. The little slave boy saw but could not taste the fine food. He compared the finely made clothes of his master's children with his own tattered tow-linen shirt. He hated whatever fortune had made his own life so different from theirs.

In 1825, when he was eight years old, Frederick's master hired him out to the Hugh Auld family in Baltimore. Douglass said that going to live in Baltimore "opened the gateway" to his later success. Sophia Auld taught him the alphabet and helped him sound out three- and four-letter words. When Hugh Auld learned what his wife was doing, he forbade her to teach Frederick another thing. He said "learning would spoil the best nigger in the world." After hearing that, Frederick was more determined than ever to learn to read and to get his hands on books. He picked up every scrap of printed paper he could find, and whatever he couldn't figure out for himself, he asked other boys on the streets of Baltimore to help him decipher.

When Frederick was 16, Hugh Auld found out that his young slave was secretly teaching a Sunday school class to young African-American children. Auld thought he had another Nat Turner on his hands, so he decided to teach Frederick a lesson. He sent a group of white men armed with sticks to break up the Sunday school class.

Shortly afterward, Auld returned Frederick to Captain Anthony. Anthony hired him out for eight months to Edward Covey, who was a professional "slave breaker," a person who tried to break the spirit of slaves by beating and humiliating them. Frederick's spirit was not so easily broken, however. After several months of abuse, he fought back and beat Covey so badly that the slave breaker never touched him again. Douglass later said that standing up to Covey completely changed his life. "I was nothing before; I was a man now."

Soon afterward, Frederick was sent to St. Michaels, Maryland, where he lived with a family who treated him kindly. But, like Harriet Tubman, he knew that his enemy was not a particular master but the system of slavery. When he tried to escape, he was sent back to the Auld family in Baltimore. This time Frederick was apprenticed as a ship caulker in his owner's shipyard. He learned quickly. While learning to be an expert caulker, he also learned about literature, geography, and arithmetic from free African Americans who lived in Baltimore. The more Frederick learned, the more he hungered for freedom.

On Monday, September 3, 1838, two years after beginning his apprenticeship, Frederick escaped slavery. One of his friends in Baltimore was a young African-American sailor. The sailor's description on his "protection" papers fit Frederick. He talked the young man into lending him both his seaman's clothes and his papers. From another friend, Anna Murray, Frederick borrowed enough money for his journey. Frederick was in love with Anna and planned to marry her as soon as he was free.

Frederick then took the train to Philadelphia, where he said he "lived more in one year than in a year of slave life." The next day he went to New York City, where he found himself in an atmosphere that was very different from the Quaker city of Philadelphia. He soon learned that he was no safer in New York than he had been in

Baltimore. Although New Yorkers could no longer own slaves, many merchants and traders made a profit on cheap goods produced by slave labor. The city teemed with agents who were looking for fugitives among the many freed slaves who lived there. Frederick felt surrounded by enemies. Still dressed as a seaman, he cautiously approached an African-American sailor, who directed him to David Ruggles. Ruggles, a member of the Underground Railroad, took Frederick in. A few days later, Frederick sent for Anna Murray, and on September 15, they became Mr. and Mrs. Frederick Augustus Washington Bailey. He returned his sailor friend's clothes and papers. He had never been so happy.

The newly married couple decided that the shipbuilding town of New Bedford, Massachusetts, would offer a ship caulker the best opportunities. Frederick was very disappointed to find that no one would hire him. White caulkers, one foreman explained, refused to work with African Americans. He ended up working for a dollar a day, which was less than he had earned as a slave. He did everything from sweeping chimneys to carrying bricks for brick-layers. Anna worked as a maid. Still, the two of them were happy and determined to be a part of their new community. They joined a nearby Methodist church only to find that they had to sit in a special section reserved for blacks. After trying several other churches, which were also segregated, they joined an all-black church.

When they had first come to New Bedford, the young couple stayed with a friend of Ruggles, Nathan Johnson, who was an agent of the Underground Railroad. Frederick Bailey needed a new name so that he could not be traced easily. Johnson suggested Frederick Douglass. Soon that name would be heard throughout the country.

Four months after moving to New Bedford, Douglass saw his first copy of William Lloyd Garrison's *Liberator*. Even though he and Anna barely had enough money to scrape by on, they became regular subscribers to the newspaper. He later wrote: "The paper became my meat and my drink. My soul was set all afire. Its sympathy for my brethren in bonds—its [scorching criticisms] of slaveholders—its faithful exposures of slavery—and its powerful attacks on the upholders of the institution—sent a thrill of joy through my soul, such as I had never felt before!"

By 1841, Douglass was chairing a meeting that had been called to oppose the Maryland Colonization Society. In August of that same year, Douglass heard Garrison speak for the first time. Douglass reacted to Garrison the way Garrison had once reacted to Lundy. Suddenly he knew what he wanted to do with his life.

A few days after first hearing Garrison speak, Douglass attended a large abolitionist meeting in Nantucket, where he was called upon to speak in front of a crowd of 500 people. In spite of having stage fright, he spoke eloquently of his experiences as a slave. When Douglass finished, Garrison asked the audience, "Have we been listening to a piece of property or a man?" The audience shouted, "A man! A man!" until the hall shook. He then asked the audience if they would allow Douglass to be taken back into slavery. "No!" they chanted. "No! No! No!"

Because of Douglass's eloquence at that meeting, Wendell Phillips, the leader of the Massachusetts Antislavery Society, asked him to become one of the society's lecturers. The job would pay a salary of $450 a year. Douglass was full of doubt about his own ability, but he couldn't refuse the offer. It was a wonderful opportunity. He would be campaigning on behalf of his people, and he would be paid more for doing so than he had received for the past year of backbreaking work. He and Anna had two children to think about now. He accepted. For the next 10 years, Douglass would be the most important lecturer and writer for the fiery Garrisonian abolitionists. This nonviolent group was later accused of bringing on the Civil War.

Harriet Tubman would never blame Garrison or Douglass, or any other abolitionist for the Civil War. She knew that slavery itself was the cause.

THE PROMISED LAND

"When I found I had crossed that line, I looked at
my hands to see if I was the same person. There
was such glory over everything; the sun came
like gold through the trees, and over the fields,
and I felt like I was in Heaven."

HARRIET TUBMAN

In 1849, Harriet Tubman made plans to escape. Unlike
Frederick Douglass, she knew nothing about geography.
In fact, she knew the names of only two northern states,
Pennsylvania and New Jersey. She could not have read a map if she
had been given one. Her only compass was the North Star. Long
ago, when she was just a child, someone had pointed out the
Drinking Gourd, the slaves' name for the Big Dipper. Here, she
was told, she would find the star that would lead her to freedom.

Tubman's first plan for escape included three of her brothers.
Since the master's death, rumors had been circulating that she and
her brothers would be sold to the next slave trader and taken south.
At first her brothers were interested in her plan, but they grew
more and more nervous as the time to escape approached. Too
many things could go wrong, they thought. It would take only one
person to betray them. They would be lucky to get out of the
county. As soon as Dr. Thompson discovered they were missing,
he would tell his slaveholding neighbors, and every white person in
Dorchester County would be looking for them. Thompson would
probably use bloodhounds. The brothers didn't think they had a

chance, but Tubman thought being taken south would make an escape even harder. They would have much farther to travel.

One evening, a friend from another part of the plantation came to the slave quarters with news that Tubman and her brothers were to be sold that very night. Faced with no other choice, Tubman decided to leave alone.

She quickly gathered her few small possessions. Legally she owned nothing, not even the clothes that she wore. Everything slaves had belonged to their masters. Tubman had made a patch-work quilt when she married John. It was the only nice thing she had ever possessed, so she took it along. As she left the quarters for the last time, she hummed "I'm bound for the promised land." This was her way of signaling good-bye to the people she loved without arousing suspicion among the whites. She then hurried toward the road to Bucktown and the house of the woman who was said to help slaves.

Tubman must have found it hard to speak when the woman opened the door. She must have had some doubts. Perhaps this was really a slave-catching woman who tricked slaves into thinking she would help them, only to sell them or return them to their masters. Tubman gave the woman her quilt, the best thing she had. The woman gave Tubman a piece of paper with some writing on it and told her how to get to the next safe house. She told Tubman to show the paper to the person who answered the door. By the time Tubman arrived at her next stop, it was morning and she was tired from her night-long journey. Instead of inviting her in, however, the woman who answered the door handed her a broom and told her to sweep the yard. Tubman wondered if she had been tricked, but she did as she was told. She later understood that the house was being watched, no one would question the presence of a slave who was sweeping a yard.

After the sun went down, the woman's husband returned. He was a farmer and had been working in the field. As soon as it was dark he loaded his wagon, hid Tubman in it, and drove to the outskirts of another town. So he wouldn't reveal the next haven to anyone who might be watching, the farmer let her out at the edge of the town. After giving her exact directions, he turned his wagon around and drove back the way he had come.

The directions were good. Tubman found the next house and several others on her long trek northward. One whole night, she followed the bank of the Choptank River. On another, she walked in the shadows at the edge of a road. On other nights, when the sky was clear, she simply followed the North Star. Along the way, she had help from both blacks and whites. Some took her in; some told her which roads to avoid; some told her which landmarks to look for. She also felt certain that God was watching over her like a kindly father. Even on the darkest nights, when she could not see the North Star, she had faith that she would be shown the right path to take. In all her life, that simple faith never left her.

Early one morning, she realized that she had crossed the Mason-Dixon Line. She was in Pennsylvania. Tubman was overcome with happiness. Years later, she said: "When I found I had crossed that line, I looked at my hands to see if I was the same person. There was such a glory over everything; the sun came like gold through the trees, and over the fields, and I felt like I was in Heaven."

Like most slaves who escaped, Tubman went North alone and with little knowledge of the world she was entering. Most fugitive slaves were male. They were young, usually single men who hoped to earn enough money in the North to buy their and their family's freedom. Because the journey from the Deep South was so dangerous, most fugitives who made it to the North came from the upper South. The upper South was made up of the states bordering the free states. These included Maryland, Delaware, Kentucky, and the part of Virginia that later became West Virginia.

Many slaves must have felt as Tubman did when they suddenly realized that they had not really reached the promised land. Long after that wonderful morning, Tubman tried to put her mixed feelings into words: "I knew of a man who was sent to the State Prison for 25 years. All these years he was always thinking of home, and counting by years, months, and days, the time till he should be free, and see his family and friends once more." Finally, the man is free. "He leaves the prison gates, he makes his way to his old home, but his old home is not there. The house in which he had dwelt in his childhood had been torn down, and a new one had been put up in its place; his family were gone, their very name was forgotten, there was no one to take him by the hand to welcome him back to life."

Tubman said this was exactly the way she felt. She had crossed that line, but there was no one to welcome her. "I was a stranger in a strange land, and my home after all was down in the old cabin quarter, with the old folks and my brothers and sisters." She vowed that she would make a home in the North and return for her people.

Tubman needed to go to Philadelphia. She had never lived in a city or even a town, but she knew that she probably wouldn't find farm work. Because she had nearly always worked outside, she could do only the most menial labor. In Philadelphia, she found a job doing kitchen work in a hotel. She earned a dollar a day, as she had in Maryland. The difference was that now, for the first time in her life, she could keep whatever she earned.

Tubman met other fugitives in the city, and they all had stories of their own journeys to freedom. Many spoke of William Still. She had heard the name before, somewhere on her journey. She knew she must meet him. Still was an African-American man, about the same age as Tubman, who knew everything there was to know about the Underground Railroad. He was the director of the Vigilance Committee, a group that helped fugitives get to Canada. There they would be welcomed as free people, out of reach of the United States' fugitive slave laws. Still was also a clerk for the Pennsylvania Anti-Slavery Society. During the darkest times, it was he who kept records of the Underground Railroad in Pennsylvania. He wrote the arrival dates of "shipments" and "passengers" from the South. More than that, he recorded the fugitives' stories. Without his work, many parts of Harriet Tubman's story could never have been verified.

William Still's own story is interesting. He was born free in New Jersey in 1821. He worked on his parents' farm until he was 23 years old. At that time he moved to Philadelphia, and within three

In posing for this picture, this escaped slave risked being returned to his former master.

years he taught himself to read and write. He started keeping his records in the early 1850s, hoping to help runaways track down other members of their families. One of the runaways he helped turned out to be his own brother, Peter, who had been kidnapped 40 years earlier and sold into slavery. Because it was illegal and dangerous to help fugitives, Still hid his records in a graveyard.

Although William Still was one of the most important figures in the antislavery movement, he wasn't alone. Tubman learned that the Quakers had been working against slavery since long before she was born. They fought the evil in every nonviolent way possible: by refusing to buy goods that had been made by slaves; by hiring African Americans; by writing antislavery literature; and by participating in the Underground Railroad. Many other people dedicated their lives and their fortunes to fighting slavery. Tubman also learned that there were other routes from slavery. These routes didn't go through Philadelphia but through the Midwest. Levi and Catherine Coffin, Quakers who lived in Indiana, helped as many as William Still did.

The knowledge that so many people were involved in the fight against slavery greatly encouraged Tubman. She knew her dream wasn't impossible. After several months of working in hotel kitchens, she found a job she liked better. She became a cook in a resort hotel in Cape May, New Jersey. Cape May, with its sea air and smaller population, must have reminded her a little of Dorchester County and home. Changing jobs because she wanted to instead of having her master decide where she would work was a new experience. Tubman was nobody's property anymore. She saved every penny she could, never losing sight of the dream of rescuing her people. But she knew that she would never be able to buy either their freedom or her own. The only thing she could do was help them escape.

One of the problems Tubman had was getting word to the people she hoped to rescue. She couldn't write, and they couldn't read. She had two ways of sending information. She could dictate her letters and allow them to be read by a trusted third party, or she could send the message through the underground network from one person to another. Tubman had been in the North for about a year when she heard that her sister Mary would soon be auctioned in Cambridge, in Dorchester County, Maryland. Mary was married to a free man, John Bowley, but he was powerless to stop the sale of his wife.

William Still would now show Tubman just how well the Underground Railroad could work. It would take too long to get Tubman all the way to Cambridge in time to save her sister. In order to rescue Mary, Tubman and Still would need to do two things: get word to her or someone in her family, and somehow get both Tubman and her sister to Baltimore. Tubman dictated a letter to be delivered to her sister's older son, Harkless Bowley, who could read. In the letter, she sent a daring plan from members of the Underground Railroad. While the auctioneer was at dinner, away from the spot where Mary waited to be sold, John would kidnap her. He would then take her and their two small children to the

home of a certain Quaker family. The Quakers would explain the rest of the plan.

John Bowley followed the instructions in the letter. As soon as it was dark, one of the Quakers took John, Mary, and the children to a small sailboat on the Choptank River. The boat contained all the supplies the family would need for their journey. Once on the river, the family rode the outgoing tide to Chesapeake Bay. From the mouth of the Choptank, they sailed the 50 miles north to Baltimore. Harkless Bowley later wrote that once his mother got to Baltimore, "Aunt Harriet had a hiding place for her. In a few days she took her and the children and several others aboard the Underground Railroad."

The trip from Baltimore to Philadelphia took almost a week. The fugitives stopped with Quaker families and free African Americans, who hid them in barns and cellars. The "stations" weren't in a straight line as those on a real railroad would be, but scattered here and there. The zigzagging route took much longer, of course, but it protected both the "passengers" and the "station-masters." Finally the family arrived in Philadelphia. They had made it to freedom. They were safe.

When Tubman rescued her sister in December 1850, she had taken her first big step toward fulfilling her dream. The North was beginning to feel a little more like home.

FUGITIVE SLAVE LAW

"I wouldn't trust Uncle Sam with my people no longer."

HARRIET TUBMAN

here were storm clouds on the horizon, from which Harriet Tubman heard only rumblings. Her abolitionist friends talked about the new Fugitive Slave Law. At that time, Tubman understood very little about law except that it never seemed to help her people. She knew that in the South the law said runaway slaves must be returned to their owners. She knew it was against the law to help them escape. She did not know that those same laws could reach across the Mason-Dixon Line. Had she been able to read Garrison's *Liberator* or Douglass's *North Star,* she would have known, as William Still did, that a terrible time was ahead for fugitive slaves in the North—and for anyone who helped them.

Southerners were angry that they could lose slaves like Tubman who escaped to the North. To them the slaves were property that they had bought. They felt the slaves should be returned like any other lost or stolen property. Slave owners thought it was just as illegal for Northerners to help fugitives as it was for Southerners to do so. The law of the United States and its Constitution were on their side. Since 1793, there had been a Fugitive Slave Law. This law gave federal judges the right to decide, without a jury, whether someone accused of being a fugitive should be returned to the person who claimed to be his or her master.

Many Northerners objected to the 1793 Fugitive Slave Law because it seemed to deny the 6th Amendment right of a trial by jury. Several northern states passed laws of their own that gave accused fugitives the right to a jury trial. Some states even provided the slaves with attorneys. In the years just before Tubman's escape from slavery, Pennsylvania and four other states passed laws that made it illegal to use local jails for the imprisonment of fugitives. These states also forbade their officials to help capture fugitives. Laws like these infuriated the Southerners, who intended to force the North to obey the old federal law.

On September 18, 1850, Congress passed a second Fugitive Slave Law. This new law did not allow suspected fugitives to have a jury trial or even to speak on their own behalf. Furthermore, their cases were not heard by real judges but by specially appointed commissioners. These commissioners were paid twice as much for returning "slaves" to their "rightful owners" as they were for releasing them. Because the local authorities hadn't helped in the past, the new law authorized United States marshals to gather a posse (a group of ordinary citizens with the power to make arrests) to catch runaways. In addition, anyone who helped a fugitive could be fined $1,000 and sent to jail.

The new law led to the abuse of both fugitive slaves and free African Americans. Any African-American man or woman could be seized, accused of being a fugitive, and sent south without a trial. The law also placed all of the participants in the Underground Railroad in greater danger.

Until the Fugitive Slave Law was passed, Harriet Tubman was in a little less danger than other runaways because she wasn't considered a very valuable slave. Dr. Thompson had intended to sell her, but he probably hadn't expected to get much for her because of her sleeping spells, head scar, and lash marks.

After the law was passed, professional slave catchers opened offices in the North and advertised their services in southern papers. Slave owners usually paid $10 to register the name and

description of a runaway and $100 if the slave was caught and returned. In some cases, the slave catchers were satisfied to pocket the $10 and forget about going after the fugitive. Unfortunately, though, many others took their jobs seriously and were always on the lookout for possible fugitives.

The threat of the new law made the Underground Railroad even more efficient than it already was. The loose network of black and white abolitionists became better organized and more secretive. They now had to be as cautious in the North as they were in the South. The law itself was probably responsible for the widespread use of the Underground Railroad code in the North. People like Harriet were called "conductors." The fugitives were referred to as "cargo," "parcels," and "passengers." Still was a "stationmaster" or "agent." The stopovers were "stations" or "depots." Even though the network had existed for a long time, it wasn't until after the Fugitive Slave Law was passed that Still began to keep and hide the careful records he later published as *The Underground Railroad*.

Tubman may not have understood the full importance of the

new law, but she was learning from Still and others how vast the antislavery network was. She wished all of her people knew. Unfortunately, no matter how many abolitionists were willing to help slaves by taking them in, feeding them, and directing them to the next stop, the only slaves who could benefit were those who knew at which door to knock. Tubman remembered how little she had known on her own trip north. Simply following the North Star wasn't enough. Now she knew a great deal more. After bringing her sister from Baltimore, she returned to her cooking job. She continued to save her money until she had enough to make her second trip south.

This time she traveled into northern Maryland to meet her brother James and two of his friends. The three men were running away from a plantation near Wilmington, a two-night walk from Philadelphia. By the time Tubman met them, the overseer and his hounds were already on their trail. The men were ready to give up. As she sometimes did, Tubman had a "hunch." Something told her they would be ambushed if they stayed on their original route. Tubman led the men to a riverbank and told them they must cross or risk capture. The men thought the river was too deep to cross by wading, and none of them could swim. Tubman stepped into the water and waded—knee-deep, hip-deep, waist-deep, then neck-deep—across the icy river, leading her passengers beyond the reach of the hounds. Afterward they learned that her hunch had been right.

In Wilmington, Tubman took James and the other two men to the home of Thomas Garrett. This was the first of many stopovers she would have with one of the railroad's most famous stationmasters. Garrett was a 60-year-old Quaker who had openly fought slavery all his life, sheltering runaways and quietly defying the angry slave owners who pursued them. He would hide the runaways in either his house or his shoe factory. When he knew they were safe, he would spirit them out of the city. The gentle Quaker was sued, fined, and even thrown into jail. Nothing discouraged him in his fight against slavery. On more than one occasion, an owner threatened him with a gun and demanded that he tell the whereabouts of a slave he had given refuge. Garrett

Fugitive slaves like this one could legally be killed by their pursuing owners.

would simply push the weapon aside and quietly say that only cowards resorted to such means. In all, Garrett helped more than 2,700 fugitives find their way north. William Lloyd Garrison called him, "one of the best men who ever walked on earth."

After her ordeal in the river, Tubman remained too sick to work for several weeks. When she finally recovered, she returned to her dollar-a-day kitchen work and began saving for a more ambitious trip. This time she would go all the way to Dorchester County to bring her husband, John Tubman, to the North. She probably thought she could persuade him by telling him about the underground network. Perhaps she thought that a man with "free" papers would make a good conductor.

In the autumn of 1851, Tubman neared Bucktown. She must have felt a mixture of happiness and sadness. For nearly two years, she had been free to come and go as she pleased, to work where she chose, and to keep what she earned. It must have been unsettling to walk again on the land where she had so long been a slave. At the same time, because she had been out of touch with all of the people she loved, her heart must have raced as she thought of seeing their faces.

If love for her husband had guided Tubman south, then certainly her heart was broken when she found him. He told her that he had no interest in going with her and that he had, in fact, taken a new wife, Caroline. Harriet Tubman had known pain all her life. A heavy heart couldn't keep her from doing the work she felt destined to do. If John Tubman didn't need her help, others did. She returned to Philadelphia with a group of fugitives, none of whom were related to her.

Tubman had now made three trips to the South and back. Already things had changed because of the new law. It was no longer enough to help fugitives get across the Mason-Dixon Line. The Fugitive Slave Law made life in the northern United States both unpleasant and risky. As Frederick Douglass had discovered long before the law was passed, the North wasn't always friendly and accepting to African-American people. And every disagreeable white person who had trouble getting a job became a potential slave catcher. As a result, William Still had to send more and more of his passengers north across another border.

Many fugitives who had already settled in the Northeast were now fleeing to Canada. Rumors of slave catchers spread through northern African-American ghettos as they once had through slave quarters. (A ghetto is a poor neighborhood that houses one ethnic or racial group.) Tubman worried that she might be leading her people out of one evil into another. She made up her mind that from then on she would take her passengers right through Pennsylvania and New York into Canada. She later told a friend, "I wouldn't trust Uncle Sam with my people no longer."

In December 1851, Tubman returned to the South for the fourth time. This time she went to rescue one of her brothers and his wife. By the time she reached Garrett's house in Wilmington, however, she had gathered nine more passengers. One was an infant. It was very difficult to move such a large group without being detected. For the sake of everyone's safety, the baby had to be given a sedative to keep it from crying.

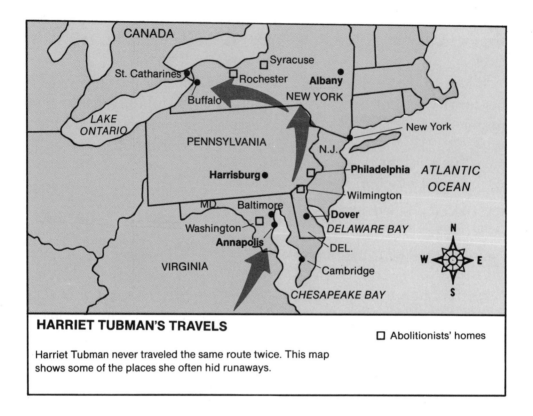

HARRIET TUBMAN'S TRAVELS

☐ Abolitionists' homes

Harriet Tubman never traveled the same route twice. This map
shows some of the places she often hid runaways.

Tubman's passengers probably felt more at ease than she did
when they knew they had crossed the line into Pennsylvania. But
she urged them on, explaining what she knew of the Fugitive Slave
Law. The December trip was cold and long. The slaves came from
milder climates, and their clothes were thin. In Rochester, New
York, the group must have stopped at Frederick Douglass's. He
later wrote, "On one occasion I had eleven fugitives at the same
time under my roof, and it was necessary for them to remain with
me until I could collect sufficient money to get them to Canada. It
was the largest number I ever had at one time, and I had some
difficulty providing so many with food and shelter. Douglass said
that the fugitives were grateful for the simplest food and, "a strip of
carpet on the floor for a bed, or a place on the straw in the barn-
loft."

The Canadian border wouldn't be the end of the story, only
another beginning.

A PARTING OF WAYS

"On a close examination of the Constitution, I
am satisfied that if strictly 'construed according
to its reading,' it is not a pro–slavery
instrument.... "

FREDERICK DOUGLASS
The North Star, February 9, 1849

Frederick Douglass moved from Lynn, Massachusetts, to Rochester, New York, in 1847. He moved to Rochester because he wanted to start his own paper. In the past, a number of African–American people had tried to keep small newspapers going. They had failed mainly because their readers were too poor to support them. Most of Douglass's white abolitionist friends, including Garrison, feared that he, too, was doomed to failure. Knowing how eloquent he was, however, supporters in Britain had urged him on. They had sent him more than $2,000 to get started.

Douglass chose Rochester because he thought it would be both a good home for his growing family and a good location for his newspaper, *The North Star.* Rochester was firmly against slavery. It had two very active antislavery societies, including the Female Anti-Slavery Society, whose members included Elizabeth Cady Stanton, Susan B. Anthony, and Sojourner Truth. All of these women were well-known speakers on the rights of women. Most abolitionists in Rochester were not Garrisonians, but they understood that slavery was a many-headed dragon. They knew that it could not be killed with a single blow. They were open-minded about other ways of fighting it.

On December 3, 1847, the first issue of *The North Star* appeared. The slogan on its masthead was, "Right is of no Sex—Truth is of no Color—God is the Father of us all, and we are all Brethren." William C. Nell, an African-American Garrisonian who had taught himself to read, was listed as the paper's publisher. Martin Delany, a brilliant man who had edited another African-American newspaper, joined Douglass as co-editor. Two white apprentices and Douglass's own children set the type and helped fold, wrap, and mail the first issue.

The reaction to that first issue was almost all good. Other abolitionists, including Garrison, praised it. And for the most part, the people of Rochester also welcomed the paper and its editors. In January, the other publishers and printers of the city invited Douglass, Delany, and Nell to a dinner in celebration of Benjamin Franklin's birthday. When the African-American men went to the dining room, however, the hotel manager refused to let them enter. The white guests threatened to leave, forcing the hotel to let Douglass and his friends join the party.

Unfortunately, the goodwill of local newspapermen wasn't enough to make *The North Star* a success. Douglass soon found that he wasn't getting enough support from anyone to keep his paper going. Followers of Garrison were disappointed to find that Douglass was backing off from some of their most important beliefs. He seemed to be siding with those Rochester abolitionists who thought the Constitution could be amended, or changed, instead of thrown out. He seemed to be suggesting that voting might change things. On the other hand, the people who favored political solutions didn't read *The North Star* because they thought Douglass was too much of a Garrisonian. These people were alarmed by any questioning of the Constitution, and they were especially afraid of the suggestion that the northern states should withdraw from the Union.

Because he loved his abolitionist friends in Boston, Douglass was saddened by their lack of support for his paper. But the thing that most disappointed him was that his readers were almost all white. He had five white subscribers for every black one. One of

Douglass's major goals in starting *The North Star* had been to reach those he referred to as 'people of color.' Douglass so wanted to have an African-American antislavery newspaper that he mortgaged his house. This means he offered it as payment in case he could not meet his debts. He spent six months of that first year traveling, trying to raise money. The paper survived through the year, but Douglass was very discouraged.

In December 1848, Douglass received a wonderful gift that raised his spirits. African-American women in Philadelphia organized a fair, much like the Boston bazaar, to benefit *The North Star*. They raised more than $100. Of course Douglass needed much more than $100 to keep the paper going, but he was especially happy to know that African-American women had had such a successful fundraiser.

Help also came from across the ocean. An English friend, Julia Griffiths, who had raised much of the money that Douglass used to start the paper, moved to the United States to manage *The North Star*. She knew that people who were completely involved with ideas and great causes weren't necessarily good at business. She didn't think Douglass should have to spend his time begging for money. She would take care of fund-raising, subscriptions, and accounting.

Julia Griffiths would help Douglass in another way. Frederick Douglass was a wonderful speaker, but he had never had a day of schooling and had done very little reading. As a result, he knew little about spelling, punctuation, and grammar. Douglass wanted his paper to be error-free because he wanted the world to know that people of color could be first-rate at whatever they did. The Englishwoman went over Douglass's writing to make sure it was in correct form. With Julia Griffiths's invaluable help, the paper was soon thriving. In June 1851, with more than 4,000 subscribers, *The North Star* merged with, or became part of, another paper. It was now called *Frederick Douglass's Paper*.

Before he became an editor, Douglass was comfortable with Garrison's claim that the Constitution supported slavery. As an editor, though, he was forced to consider opposing points of view.

He read the Constitution for himself and decided that, in spirit at least, it really did not support slavery.

Colonization was less of an issue now than it had been, because it had proved impractical. But the colonizationists' belief that blacks shouldn't live and work beside whites remained. This belief expressed itself in many forms of segregation that had bothered Douglass ever since he came North.

As a young man Douglass had been disappointed to find that even though he was free, his dark skin made him an object of scorn. He had been unable to work as a caulker. He had not been allowed to sit among the white people in church. On his trip to England, he had been forced to travel in steerage, the cheapest section, while his white traveling companions sailed first-class.

When he traveled, Douglass always avoided Jim Crow cars. These were the railroad cars in which African Americans were forced to ride. He made it a rule to seat himself in the regular cars.

But as soon as he sat down, the conductor would approach him to explain that he was in the wrong car. Douglass always refused to move and was usually dragged away, sometimes getting roughed up on his way to the black car.

As the editor of a black newspaper, Douglass was forced to think about incidents like this and what they meant for his people. He wanted to see an end to the practice of Jim Crow. He did not believe that freed slaves should be forced to go to Liberia, and he did not believe that African-American people should have to move to Canada in order to be treated decently. He believed strongly that if the slaves of the South were to be free, the freed African Americans of the North would first have to be educated and made aware of the issues that touched their lives.

Douglass's new beliefs caused a break between him and his old friend Garrison. Garrison thought Douglass was ungrateful for the help he had given him. What Garrison failed to understand was that even though Douglass admired him, he had to go in his own direction. The split between the two friends strengthened Douglass's support. By the time Tubman and her first group of refugees came through Rochester, Douglass was probably the most influential African American in the United States.

FREE AT LAST

"Who can speak the blessedness of that first day
of Freedom?...To move, speak, and breathe, go
out and come in, unwatched and free from
danger!"

HARRIET BEECHER STOWE
Uncle Tom's Cabin

When Tubman and her 11 passengers left Rochester, New York, they still had to travel another 60 miles or so to the town of St. Catharines in Canada. To enter Canada, they had to cross a bridge that was suspended over Niagara Falls. Nothing any of the slaves had ever seen could have equaled that experience. As they listened to the roar of the falls and walked through the rising mist, they must have felt that they were crossing into another world rather than just another country.

From the border, the tattered group still had many miles to walk before reaching St. Catharines. William Still had referred Tubman to Hiram Wilson, an African-American minister who helped fugitives settle in Canada. She needed all the help she could get. Her people were frostbitten and hungry. Wilson provided them with temporary shelter and a way to survive the winter. The refugees would earn their keep by cutting wood in the nearby forest.

Even though the winter was harsh—especially for people who were used to the mild Maryland climate—Tubman, her brother, and the others enjoyed their first taste of true freedom. In 1833, slavery was forbidden in Canada, as in all of Britain. Canada's new laws gave everyone equal rights. African-American people could own property, serve on juries, and run for political office. In cities big enough to have public schools, blacks could attend along with whites. There were about 30,000 African-American people in this part of Canada at this time. Most of them were fugitives from the United States.

Ex-slaves in Canada did face one problem they also had in the United States, however. People who had lived their entire lives on farms usually ended up in the larger cities, where there wasn't enough work for them. Without education or special skills, they had to do menial work and live in the poorest, most crowded sections of town.

St. Catharines, on the south shore of Lake Ontario, had a population of 6,000. Seven hundred were African Americans. Even though it was a small town, it was modern for those times. It had a telegraph line and a railroad. The Welland Canal, which connects Lake Erie and Lake Ontario, made St. Catharines a port town. This made jobs more plentiful and varied here than they were in most towns. Most of St. Catharines's people—black and white— lived in small, neat wooden houses. Education was available to everyone, and both blacks and whites had a say in the town government.

Here African-American refugees found true opportunity. In the spring, Tubman saw African-American people clearing their own land and planting their own crops. Tubman wanted to make her own home in St. Catharines, but she also wanted all of her people to find out what it was like to be part of such a community.

Tubman knew that her friends in the northern United States were doing all they could to bring an end to slavery. Most of the issues were clear to her. She thought colonization was a bad idea. She didn't want her people sent back to Africa because she knew that the United States had become rich partly because of the labor and sacrifice of the African Americans. The land was as much theirs as anyone's. She also knew that laws could be even stronger than chains for binding people to slavery. But she didn't understand who was right about the Constitution. She would never be able to read it for herself, so she did not really understand the argument between Douglass and Garrison. All she knew was that in their own ways, both men were fighting for the very thing for which she herself had been fighting.

What she did understand was the power of the Underground Railroad. She knew that whenever she brought away a slave, she wasn't just freeing another human being; she was also taking money away from a master. The plantation owners had invested a large part of their wealth in slaves. Tubman and others who worked with the Underground Railroad believed that if they ruined enough owners, slavery would soon become a very bad investment.

In that winter of 1852, Tubman knew that her job was just beginning. No matter how promising St. Catharines was, the Underground Railroad must keep on rolling. Her brother and the others were free, ready to make their own way in Canada. Tubman needed cash to continue her work. In the spring, she left for Cape May to work in homes and resort hotels. She saved all the money she earned during the vacation season and returned to Maryland to rescue nine more fugitives. By now, Tubman had led so many people from the "land of Egypt" to freedom that she was becoming known as "Moses." Unfortunately, she wasn't known only among the slaves. The rewards for her capture had grown as fast as her reputation. At one time plantation owners offered a total of $40,000 for her capture. The state of Maryland offered another $12,000.

From 1852 to 1857, while Tubman lived in St. Catharines, she made a total of 11 trips into Maryland. Many bits and pieces of those trips have become part of the legend of Harriet Tubman. One of the most famous stories concerns a passenger who panicked and wanted to turn back. Tubman didn't want him to leave the group because even if he returned safely to his old master, he could be tortured until he told what he knew. Not only would that endanger her and the other passengers, but it would also reveal the identities of the good people who had helped them escape. The unwilling passenger changed his mind only when Tubman pointed a gun at his head and told him to keep walking, saying that dead folks told

Harriet Tubman, herself an escaped slave, risked capture to bring other slaves north to freedom.

no tales. She had more than one exhausted or fainthearted passenger in the 19 trips she made from the South. She threatened each the same way.

Once Tubman had a fugitive whose master had already posted a large reward for him. His scars made him easy to identify. She hired a black accomplice (someone who helps a lawbreaker) to follow the runaway's master at a safe distance, removing any posters he tacked up. Usually Tubman avoided such problems by starting north on a Saturday night. On most Maryland plantations the field hands didn't work on Sundays, which meant that slaves who escaped the night before had one extra night in which to travel before the overseer missed them.

On one of Tubman's most daring rescues, she had to go into a town near the house of her former master. She pretended to be an old woman, bent and crippled. She bought two live chickens, which she carried by a cord tied around their legs. When she saw her master's son approaching, she let the chickens go. They flew off in opposite directions, amusing bystanders and distracting the young man. The confusion provided the perfect cover for the "old woman" to make her escape.

In 1854, Tubman planned to rescue three more of her brothers from Dorchester County. First, she needed to let them know that she was coming. She dictated a letter that said: "Read my letter to the old folks, and give my love to them, and tell my brothers to be always watching unto prayer, and when the good ship of Zion comes along, to be ready to step aboard." Tubman sent the letter to Jacob Jackson, a free African-American member of the Underground Railroad who knew how to read. Slaves often used a code based on the Bible. They did this whether they were singing in the fields or trying to send a message to someone on another plantation. Postal authorities, who read mail that came from the North, suspected secret messages but seldom understood them.

When the local postmaster read the letter addressed to Jacob Jackson, he called him in and asked him to explain. Jackson read the letter and knew immediately what it meant, but he said, "That letter can't be meant for me. I can't make head or tail of it." His

pretense convinced the postmaster that it was all a mistake. The postmaster was probably relieved as he watched Jackson disappear. He did not guess that Jackson went immediately to inform Benjamin, Robert, and Henry Ross that Moses was on her way.

The brothers must have thought that "the good ship Zion" really was about to arrive—and just in time. A slave trader was coming through Bucktown the following Monday, the day after Christmas. Dr. Thompson planned to sell them just as he had two of their brothers. Within a few days of the letter to Jackson, Tubman and the Underground Railroad sent another message to the brothers. They must be ready to leave after sundown on the Friday night before Christmas. Their first stop would be the cabin of their parents, Rit and Ben, who now lived in Caroline County, nearly 40 miles north. There was no time to waste. They must use Christmas Day to get out of Dr. Thompson's reach. This wouldn't be easy, because he owned a great deal of property in both counties.

Tubman arrived at dusk, just as she had promised she would. Three more slaves, John Chase, Peter Jackson, and Jane Kane, had joined the brothers. The group had far to travel in a very short time, but Tubman knew they could make it. Unfortunately, just as they were ready to leave, her brother Henry was called back to his cabin. His wife was having a baby. He refused to leave her until the baby was born. When he asked the rest of them to wait, Tubman said no. They would have to stick to their plan, even if it meant leaving him behind. With the party of five, she set off for Caroline County.

That wasn't the only example of Tubman's soldierlike discipline. On Christmas Eve, when they got near her parents' cabin, she commanded her brothers to hide with her in a nearby feed shed. She hadn't seen Rit and Ben for five years, and she knew that her mother had planned a wonderful Christmas meal for the three brothers and their families. Rit would roast the pig she had raised that year and bake sweet potatoes and cornbread, happily thinking of seeing her sons. But she would see none of her children that Christmas.

Tubman knew that neither Rit nor Ben would stand up well to questioning. They were honest, religious people who couldn't lie very well. Tubman came up with a plan that made it unnecessary for either of her parents to lie. Rit would not even know that her children had been so close. She sent John Chase and Peter Jackson to call Ben out of the cabin. When he was out of Rit's earshot, the men told him about the escape plan and asked him for food. They explained to him why he couldn't visit with his children and warned him not to tell Rit that her sons and daughter were hiding in the shed. She was to know nothing of the escape until Thompson's men told her.

Ben brought the group food during the night and even walked blindfolded with them as they left the Thompson farm. He kept his promise not to tell Rit. A few days later, when the slave hunters came looking for the Ross brothers, Ben was able to say honestly that he hadn't seen any of them. Rit reported, with true sadness, that she hadn't seen them—even on Christmas after she had prepared such a fine dinner for them.

Toward morning, Henry caught up with them. Desperate not to be sold south, he had left his wife and newborn child behind. He planned to return for them later.

Three days later, Tubman and her six passengers arrived at Thomas Garrett's house in Wilmington, Delaware. He wrote J. Miller McKim, the next underground agent on the trip north, "Harriet, and one of the men had worn their shoes off their feet and I gave them two dollars to help fit them out, and directed a carriage to be hired at my expense, to take them out." They stopped with William Still in Philadelphia, then continued toward St. Catharines, where they arrived in early January of 1855.

HARRIET BEECHER STOWE

"They live in nice New England homes, clean, sweet-smelling, shut up in libraries, writing books which ease their hearts of bitterness against us."

MARY BOKIN CHESTNUT
Diary from Dixie

A t about the time Harriet Tubman first made her way to Canada, another Harriet, Harriet Beecher Stowe, wrote a series of stories for the *National Era*. The serial, *Uncle Tom's Cabin,* was a story about slavery. It was so popular that in 1852, it was republished as a novel. By the time the Civil War started, Stowe's book was outselling every other book except the Bible. The book's antislavery message reached into a hundred times as many homes as Garrison's *Liberator* and *Frederick Douglass's Paper* had. More important, it reached ordinary readers who were not already involved in the battle against slavery.

Harriet Beecher Stowe's life was very different from Harriet Tubman's. Born in Litchfield, Connecticut, in 1811, she grew up surrounded by books and highly educated people. When she was eight years old, she started school at Litchfield Female Academy. There she learned needlework, music, and drawing, as many young women did. She also learned Latin, Greek, and science.

Even as a child, Harriet showed promise as a writer. When she was 11, she wrote a very fine essay on the nature of the soul that her

Harriet Beecher Stowe, who wrote *Uncle Tom's Cabin* to protest the injustice of slavery.

teacher read aloud to the large audience attending Litchfield's annual awards ceremony. Lyman Beecher was extremely proud when he learned that his own daughter was the author of the essay. He once said that she would have made a wonderful minister if she had only been a boy.

After Litchfield, Harriet attended Hartford Female Academy, which her sister Catharine had founded. Colleges did not admit women in those times, so Harriet's formal education ended when she finished at Hartford. Still, she received a much better education than did most people of her time. After graduating, she became a teacher at her sister's school.

From her youth, Harriet Beecher was exposed to the many different views of the abolitionists. Her father was a colonizationist. Her brother Edward leaned more toward the Garrisonians. When she was 18, she heard William Lloyd Garrison deliver the Fourth of July sermon at a church in Boston. It was like no other Fourth of July message she had ever heard. Garrison said, "The Fourth of July is the worst and most disastrous day in the whole three hundred and sixty-five." He said that the day no longer celebrated the rights of human beings, but was just an occasion for fireworks, drunkenness, and high-flown words. He said that as long as people held slaves, "our destruction is not only possible but certain."

Garrison's angry words made Harriet think. She had agreed with her father that slavery was wrong, and that all slaves should be freed and given help to establish a home in Liberia. But she hadn't thought of slavery as an urgent problem. When she was born, New Englanders owned more than 10,000 slaves. Those slaves were now free, and she had assumed that slavery in the South was also declining. Garrison made her realize that slavery was a growing problem in America, that there were now more than twice as many slaves in the United States as there had been at the end of the Revolutionary War.

Harriet Beecher wasn't quite 20 when she and most of her family moved west. Her father had been asked to become the president of Lane Theological Seminary in Cincinnati, Ohio. He took his adult daughters and eight other family members with him.

In 1833, Harriet and Catharine opened the Western Female Institute in downtown Cincinnati. Cincinnati was very different from either the peaceful New England towns Harriet had grown up in or the old, established city of Boston. The first thing Harriet noticed about the Ohio town was its many large, handsome brick houses. The next thing she noticed was the poor area of town, where pigs roamed the streets and people lived in shacks. In the winter, terrible fires swept through this area. In the summer, badly drained streets poisoned the water supply and caused deadly epidemics of cholera that spread through the entire city.

The poorest section of town was called Little Africa. Here African-American people who had been freed from slavery lived in extreme poverty. They were uneducated, had few skills, and little hope. The women did domestic work; the men hauled bricks, loaded boats, and worked in the city's slaughterhouses. The little money they made often went to buy the freedom of family members who were still slaves.

Theodore Weld, one of the ministry students at Lane Seminary, was a follower of Garrison. He hoped to get other students at Lane involved in the fight against slavery. In 1834, he organized a series of talks by abolitionists with differing points of view. Lyman Beecher argued for colonization. Weld argued that the African-American people were American citizens who should be freed at once. Weld and his followers did more than argue, however. They founded the Lane Anti-Slavery Society. The society opened a school in the middle of Little Africa for African-American people of all ages and both sexes. They hired five young women from New York to teach the women and children. The seminary students themselves gave lectures on science and literature and held nightly classes to teach adults how to read. They stayed overnight in the homes of their students, and the African-American students visited the seminary. The young men thought they were being good Christians, but many people in town saw them as dangerous revolutionaries.

When the board of trustees of Lane Seminary found out what the students were doing, its members were furious. In the summer, while the students were away, the board abolished the Lane Anti-Slavery Society. Lyman Beecher did not object to the board's action. He was against slavery, but he believed that the change should come about slowly. Both Harriet and Catharine Beecher went along with their father's point of view without questioning it, but Harriet still remembered Garrison's words in that Fourth of July sermon.

Weld and most of his followers left Lane. The trustees and Lyman Beecher were happy to see them go, but some powerful abolitionists weren't. Arthur and Lewis Tappan, the wealthy New York abolitionists, refused to give any more money to the college. Only a few students came to replace the young men who left. Lyman Beecher and his school were in trouble.

Harriet Beecher continued to teach until 1835, when she married Calvin Stowe, the widower of her closest friend. For a while after she stopped teaching, Harriet had more time to write. She read abolitionist papers and attended lectures by famous antislavery speakers. She still didn't agree completely with Weld and Garrison, but she believed that all sides had a right to be heard. When a new Garrisonian, James Gillespie Birney, came to town and started a new antislavery society, she took his side. When Birney tried to start an abolitionist newspaper in Cincinnati, an angry mob destroyed his press. It then decided to lynch Birney. When the enraged mob reached his home, he wasn't there, so it turned its fury on Little Africa. The would-be lynch mob terrorized the innocent blacks by smashing windows, ripping doors from their hinges, and chasing the people into the streets.

Harriet Stowe finally began to understand that slavery wasn't a distant issue. When one of Edward's closest friends, Elijah Lovejoy, was shot by a mob for his abolitionist writings, Harriet knew she must join the fight. She still didn't know what she could do, though. She was a middle-class housewife who thought her first duty was to her home. Over the next several years, she would give birth to six children.

But in 1840, Harriet Stowe read an article that haunted her for many years. The Southern abolitionist Sarah Grimké had written the supposedly true story of a slave's death. According to the story,

Sarah Grimké, whose tale of an abused slave moved Harriet Beecher Stowe to write *Uncle Tom's Cabin*.

the slave's master was entertaining a guest who had suggested that black people didn't have a sincere interest in the Christian religion. He thought they only pretended to be devout. The host disagreed with his guest and said that he would prove to him that a slave's religious devotion could be as true as a white man's. The master sent for Tom, a particularly obedient slave whom he knew to be deeply religious. He demanded that the slave admit that he didn't believe in God. The slave said that he couldn't deny his belief in his Savior. The master whipped him with a cowhide, but the slave would not deny his belief in God. Again and again the master whipped him. The master kept saying, "Just say what I told you to, and I'll turn you loose." But Tom remained silent. When he had been lashed more than 200 times with the cowhide, the slave died.

Harriet Stowe was so troubled by the story that she couldn't sleep. She was more convinced than ever that she must do something. But she already had her hands full with her growing family. Stowe was teaching her children in her home. She began to invite local African-American children to join the lessons. One day one of the children didn't come to class. Later that day, the child's mother came to the Stowes' door to explain what had happened. It seemed that although the mother herself was free, the child had not been emancipated. When the mother's former master died, the administrator of his estate came to Ohio and seized the child to sell at auction. Harriet Stowe was horrified. The Stowes and their friends quickly raised enough money to buy the child, but Harriet couldn't help thinking how terrible it would be to lose a child.

She would soon learn. In 1848, a cholera epidemic struck Cincinnati. More than 100 people died every day. Ministers blamed the epidemic on God's anger and asked everyone in the city to fast and pray on July 3. On that same day, 120 people were buried. A week later, the Stowes' 18-month-old son, Samuel Charles, became ill. He died after two weeks.

Harriet Stowe wrote to her husband, who was in New England, that most houses in the city had been touched by death. She thought it was like the biblical plague of Egypt, where the firstborn in every house died because the pharaoh held the Jews as slaves. She thought that she herself had been punished for failing to do something about the evil of slavery in her own time.

In the spring, after Calvin Stowe returned home, the Stowes moved to Maine. While sitting in church one day, Harriet Stowe's mind wandered from the sermon to the story Sarah Grimké had written. In her mind, she could see Tom being whipped. At last she knew what she must do. She must write a story that would force its readers to see for themselves how wrong slavery was.

Uncle Tom's Cabin was that story. Many American writers with firsthand knowledge could probably have written a novel about slavery, but no one did. It took a New England housewife who had only been in the South for one brief visit to write the most influential book of the century.

UNCLE TOM'S CABIN;

OR,

LIFE AMONG THE LOWLY.

BY

HARRIET BEECHER STOWE.

VOL. I.

BOSTON:
JOHN P. JEWETT & COMPANY.
CLEVELAND, OHIO:
JEWETT, PROCTOR & WORTHINGTON.
1852.

The original cover of *Uncle Tom's Cabin*, one of the most influential novels ever written.

REIGN OF TERROR

"Slavery always has, and always will, produce
insurrections wherever it exists, because it is
a violation of the natural order of things,
and no human power can much longer
perpetuate it. ... "

ANGELINA GRIMKÉ
The Anti-Slavery Examiner, September 1836

W ithin the next few years, people all over the world had read *Uncle Tom's Cabin.* In the United States, much to Harriet Beecher Stowe's disgust, stage versions of her book appeared everywhere. In these "Tom plays," as they were called, white people played all the parts. They turned the characters of Stowe's book into black-faced clowns. Once when Harriet Tubman was in Philadelphia, one of her friends told her she should go to see *Uncle Tom's Cabin.* She answered, "I haven't got the heart to go and see the sufferings of my people played on the stage." She did have the heart to see and battle the real thing, however.

In the spring of 1857, Tubman set out on what many believe was her most daring rescue. She had heard that her elderly father, Ben Ross, was in trouble. She had long dreamed of rescuing her parents, but she knew the 300-mile trip to Canada would be extremely difficult for them. They might not even be able to walk out of Caroline County. Tubman decided they wouldn't have to. She raised enough money from northern abolitionists to buy a train ticket for herself. She traveled in broad daylight, believing that an African-American woman traveling toward the South would not

Harriet Tubman brought these members of her family north along the
Underground Railroad.

arouse suspicion in anyone. When she reached Caroline County,
she bought an old horse and a pair of wheels on an axle. She laid a
board along the axle for a seat and hung a second board from the
axle for a footrest. She then hitched the horse to her "buggy" with
rope and a straw collar. With this contraption, she brought her
parents out of Caroline County in Maryland, all the way to
Wilmington, Delaware. In Wilmington, she put the old people on a
railroad car, then delivered the horse and buggy to Thomas
Garrett. He gave her enough money to complete the trip to
Canada. When she was well on her way, Garrett sold the horse and
sent her the cash.

In Philadelphia, William Still was surprised to see that such old
people had survived an escape. Benjamin Ross told Still that he and
Rit were looking forward to seeing some of their children who
now lived in the North. Even though they were old and had few
years left to live, the Rosses were glad to know that they would live
out their lives as free people.

The rescue of her parents showed how daring Tubman had become. She no longer had to creep through the woods at night. She was so familiar with both the enemy and the underground that she knew when the patrollers made their rounds, where they looked, and what roads they followed. In her many trips, she had met most of the agents of the eastern network.

On each journey, she chose a slightly different route. From Dorchester County in Maryland, she usually went to Delaware. Sometimes she took her passengers to Cooper House in Camden, which had a secret bunk room above the kitchen. At other times she stopped in Odessa at the Quaker meeting house, which had a loft where runaways hid. On the way north, her passengers might hide in a farmer's "potato hole"—a rough cellar for storing vegetables. Of course, Tubman stopped again and again at Thomas Garrett's in Wilmington, where her passengers sometimes hid in a secret room at his shoe factory.

Once her people had crossed into Pennsylvania, Tubman herself often turned back after telling the runaways how to find their way to J. M. McKim, William Still, or James E. Mason. Mason, an African-American educator, wrote that Moses did much of her work in the dangerous area near the Mason-Dixon Line, where the "crack of the slaveholder's lash repeatedly resounded in her ears."

She knew nearly every agent—black and white, rich and poor— and just about every hiding place on the route from Dorchester County to the Canadian border. The Reverend J. W. Loguen, an African-American minister in Syracuse, New York, was one of her friends. Gerrit Smith, the wealthy white reformer who lived in Peterboro, New York, also befriended her. William H. Seward, who later became Lincoln's secretary of state, was her good friend. It's not surprising, then, that John Brown went to Harriet Tubman for help when he planned his rebellion.

John Brown was a radical abolitionist. He wanted to see the system of slavery ended immediately, and he was willing to resort to violence to achieve his goal. In years past, while trying to keep Kansas a free state, Brown and his men had led bloody raids on Kansas farms in which many slaveholders were killed. In April

Abolitionist John Brown captured but failed to hold the arsenal at Harpers Ferry, Virginia.

1858, he was ready to start a major uprising against slaveholders in Virginia. He claimed that he did not intend to overthrow the United States government, that he wanted only to destroy slavery and replace the constitution that had allowed it.

Brown had many white sponsors in the Northeast, but he knew that he needed a strong African-American leader at his side if he was to get the support of other African Americans. Everywhere he went, Brown heard about Tubman's bravery and her soldierlike qualities. He wondered if she might be the African-American leader he was looking for. In April 1858, Brown visited St. Catharines, where he asked J. W. Loguen to introduce him to this great woman. When he met Tubman, Brown was so struck by her intelligence and bearing that he just said, over and over, "General Tubman. General Tubman. General Tubman." From that first meeting, he always referred to her as "General Tubman." He said that she was "one of the best and bravest persons on this continent."

Brown told her of his plan to invade Virginia. He said he would need to recruit slaves and to know where his rebels could hide. He told her he wanted to capture the government arsenal at Harpers Ferry and take control of the town. He explained that the town was only 8 miles from Baltimore and 57 miles from Washington. Further, it was located at the spot where the Shenandoah and Potomac rivers flow together to form one river. At this place there were two bridges. One was a covered bridge where the Baltimore and Ohio Railroad crossed the river to connect with the Winchester and Harpers Ferry Railroad. By controlling that spot, John Brown's army would be able to disrupt life in both Washington and Baltimore. And, Brown said, the nearby mountains would offer the raiders many hiding places.

Tubman listened carefully. She liked the plan. She gave Brown the information he wanted about the Underground Railroad in Maryland and Delaware, and she quickly moved to gather recruits. Brown had originally planned to attack the Harpers Ferry arsenal in the spring of 1858. His supporters were ready to go forward, but Brown kept changing his plans. By 1859, some of Tubman's recruits had begun to have second thoughts. She suggested to Brown that he attack the armory at Harpers Ferry on July 4. On this day they would catch the town off guard, but Tubman also liked the symbolism. She wanted to make Independence Day truly worth celebrating.

Brown seemed to listen to her. He moved some of his men into Virginia in late June. On July 3, he rode into Harpers Ferry but decided that he could not capture the well-guarded arsenal. He needed more troops, and he needed "the General." He sent for Tubman, but she was not in St. Catharines. He learned that she and her parents had moved to Auburn, New York. When Brown tried to reach her there, her parents told his messenger that she was away. Word finally came back to him that Tubman was in New Bedford,

Harpers Ferry, Virginia, scene of the failed rebellion.

Massachusetts. She was sick and unable to travel. Brown was very disappointed. Without Tubman, he could expect little support from African Americans. The fugitive slaves he had counted on had been out of touch with his changing plans. Some even thought he had given up the plan altogether.

Brown tried to talk Frederick Douglass into joining him at Harpers Ferry, but Douglass refused. He was neither a soldier nor a strategist nor a skilled military leader. Finally, after realizing that he wasn't going to have an African-American leader, Brown set the date of attack for October 24. His recruits from New England and Canada were to join him just outside of Harpers Ferry. Again, with most of his army still on its way, he changed his mind. On October 16, 1859, eight days earlier than he had planned, John Brown and 22 men attacked Harpers Ferry. They seized the arsenal, the bridges, and the town itself.

The fight didn't end with the capture of Harpers Ferry, however. The rebels would have to either defend what they had seized or take their captured guns and ammunition and run, hiding in the mountains in order to carry on future raids. Instead, Brown freed slaves, took hostages, and stayed in town. The next morning, he sent for 45 hotel breakfasts for his men and hostages. While he and his men wasted time, news of the attack spread. Virginia assembled militia men. The federal government sent marines.

Within two days, Brown and his small force were defeated. Two of his sons were killed. Brown was tried and convicted of treason. He was hanged on December 2, 1859. Brown had been right about at least one thing: He had needed Harriet Tubman.

Harpers Ferry and the events that followed brought the North and the South to the edge of war. Hanging John Brown turned him into a martyr. He had, after all, been hanged because he chose to act on his beliefs. Even nonviolent abolitionists who had always thought Brown was a little crazy were suddenly forced to support what he had done. The support he received from such prominent New Englanders as Thomas Wentworth Higginson, Ralph Waldo Emerson, and Henry David Thoreau enraged Southerners.

Garrison called the reaction in the South "the new reign of terror." Northerners traveling in the South were all suspected of being enemies. Some were arrested and asked, "Did you know old Brown, the insurrectionist?" A suspicious answer might get the traveler tarred and feathered. A minister from North Carolina was thrown into a Texas jail and given 70 lashes for preaching that slaves should be treated kindly. Another man, who praised John Brown, was pushed off a moving train.

The North had the opposite reaction. A few months after John Brown's death, Harriet Tubman was passing through Troy, New York. The whole town seemed ready to erupt into a riot. A fugitive slave, Charles Nalle, was being held by federal marshals for return to his owner under the Fugitive Slave Law. Abolitionists had a plan. A hostile crowd, hoping for a chance to free Nalle, gathered outside the federal courthouse. As she had done before, Tubman twisted herself into the form of a pitiful old woman. Bent over and hobbling, she worked her way through the crowd, leaning on two other African-American women. When they reached the court-room where Nalle was being held, they waited at the door. As the guards led the prisoner from the room, the "old woman" became strong and agile.

She and her companions grabbed Nalle and pulled him away from the guards. They then led him toward the river and a waiting ferry, where a large part of the crowd followed him aboard to make sure he wasn't recaptured on the other side of the river. In spite of the crowd's protection, as soon as the boat reached the other shore, Nalle was seized and taken to the judge's office. Again, Tubman and her followers grabbed him. This time they put him on a wagon that carried him out of town.

A short time after this incident, Tubman told John Brown's old friend, Frank B. Sanborn, that no matter how much people talked about peace, she knew there was going to be a war.

14

WAR

"'A house divided against itself cannot stand.' I
believe this government cannot endure
permanently, half slave and half free."

ABRAHAM LINCOLN

n June 1, 1860, Harriet Tubman spoke to a large Boston
audience. As Garrison reported on the event in the
Liberator: "[A colored woman of the name of Moses] told
the story of her adventures in a modest, but quaint and amusing
style which won much applause." John Bell Robinson, a proslavery writer, had a different view of Moses and her audience. He
wrote that the event was insulting to the South. He was angry that
"a poor weak-minded negro woman, in trampling on the rights of
the South" had made the audience "laugh and shout." He said that
the "deluded negress" had taken over $50,000 worth of property
from southern slaveholders. Robinson wrote that the only thing the
South could do was secede from a union that refused to protect its
rights.

Tubman wasn't satisfied with talking of past adventures, however. In December 1860, a few weeks after Abraham Lincoln was
elected president of the United States, Moses made her last rescue
trip into Maryland. She brought out seven people, including two
little girls and an infant. Her New England friends had raised funds
for the trip, and she received the usual help from Thomas Garrett,

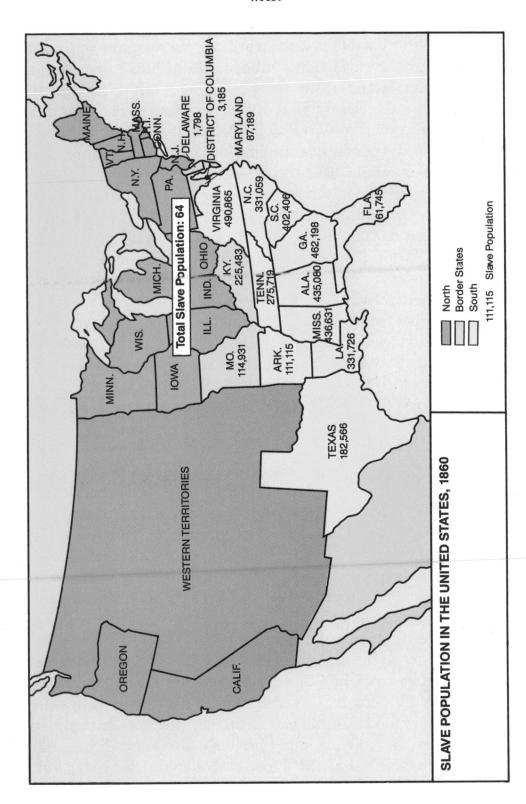

SLAVE POPULATION IN THE UNITED STATES, 1860

Legend:
- North
- Border States
- South

111,115 Slave Population

Total Slave Population: 64

WESTERN TERRITORIES

OREGON
CALIF.
TEXAS 182,566
MINN.
IOWA
MO. 114,931
ARK. 111,115
LA. 331,726
MISS. 436,631
WIS.
ILL.
IND.
OHIO
KY. 225,483
TENN. 275,719
ALA. 435,080
MICH.
N.Y.
PA.
VT.
N.H.
MASS.
R.I.
CONN.
N.J.
MAINE
DELAWARE 1,798
DISTRICT OF COLUMBIA 3,185
MARYLAND 87,189
VIRGINIA 490,865
N.C. 331,059
S.C. 402,406
GA. 462,198
FLA. 61,745

but it was Tubman herself who took the great risk. After seeing Tubman, Garrett wrote that the trip from Wilmington was more dangerous than ever. He gave Tubman $10 to hire a man with a carriage who would drive the passengers from New Castle, Delaware, to Chester County in Pennsylvania. He was still worried, however. He wrote William Still that "poor, worthless wretches" were constantly patrolling the roads that Tubman and her passengers would have to take from Wilmington. "Yet," he wrote, "as it is Harriet, who seems to have had a special angel to guard her on her journey of mercy, I have hope." That rescue was the last Tubman would make for the Underground Railroad. She had made 19 trips, rescued more than 300 people, and never lost a single passenger.

When she returned to her home in Auburn, New York, her friends told her that she was in very serious danger. They escorted her to Canada. South Carolina had seceded from the Union on December 20, 1860. War was almost certain. Tubman's abolitionist friends were afraid that if she stayed in the United States, she would be used as part of a compromise, or agreement, with the South. For instance, northern politicians might promise to deliver her to the governor of Maryland to keep his state from seceding.

Tubman stayed in Canada until the spring of 1861. By mid-February of that year, six more states in the Deep South had seceded. They had joined South Carolina in organizing the Confederate States of America. They inaugurated Jefferson Davis president on February 18. The Confederate states claimed all forts and other U.S. property within their boundaries as their own. Lincoln refused to recognize their claims or abandon federal land. He believed that abandoning the posts would be the same as saying the Confederate states had a right to them.

Fort Sumter, at the mouth of Charleston Bay in South Carolina, had been under attack by Confederate forces for three months, ever since South Carolina had seceded. The U.S. troops there were running out of food. Lincoln was afraid they might be starved into surrender, so he asked South Carolina's Governor Pickens for permission to send a shipload of food and other supplies to the fort.

Pickens told Jefferson Davis of Lincoln's request. Instead of granting the request, Davis ordered General P. G. T. Beauregard to take Fort Sumter. The attack on Fort Sumter on April 12, 1861, started one of the bloodiest wars in the history of the United States. Lincoln's tough stand had nothing to do with the issue of slavery, however. His main concern was preserving the Union.

Soon after the war started, Tubman may have worked as a nurse in the "contraband" hospital at Fortress Monroe, Virginia. The word *contraband* usually refers to illegal property, but during the Civil War it referred to slaves who escaped to the protection of the Union army. General Benjamin Franklin Butler coined the term at Fortress Monroe when a Virginia slave owner asked him to return three runaway slaves. He refused, saying that the slaves were "the contraband of war." This term meant that the escaped slaves were not truly free but were still thought of as property.

Douglass, Garrison, and other abolitionists called for Lincoln to free the slaves outright. When she returned to the North, Tubman criticized Lincoln, saying, "They may send the flower of their young men down South, to die of fever in the summer and the

Slaves, left behind by Southerners fleeing the Union Army, are educated at a contraband school.

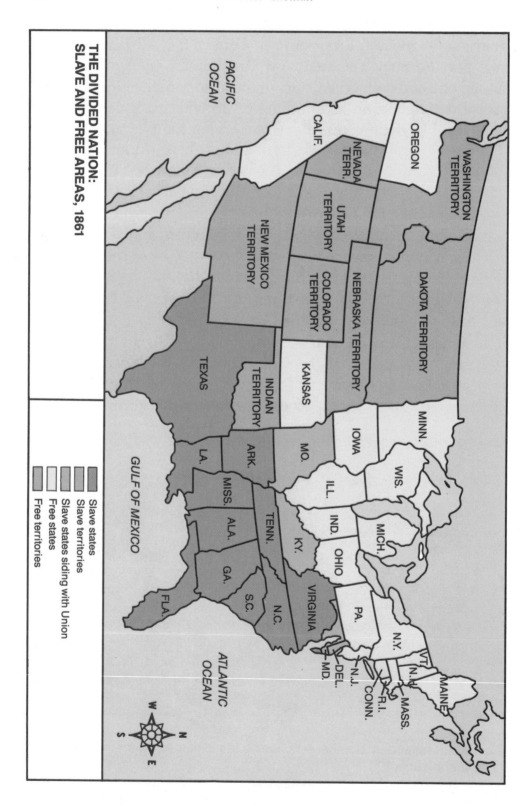

THE DIVIDED NATION:
SLAVE AND FREE AREAS, 1861

Slave states
Slave territories
Slave states siding with Union
Free states
Free territories

ague in the winter. They may send them one year, two year, three year, till they tire of sending or till they use up the young men. All of no use." Tubman continued, "God won't let Mister Lincoln beat the South until he does the right thing. Mister Lincoln, he is a great man, and I am a poor Negro: but this Negro can tell Mister Lincoln how to save the money and young men. He can do it by setting the Negroes free."

By 1862, the largest contraband settlements were in Beaufort and Hilton Head, South Carolina. A large number of slaves had been left behind on plantations when the owners fled from the Union army. The Union army now needed help. It wanted the slaves to take control of the abandoned plantations, govern themselves, and cultivate the land.

Abolitionists raised money to send teachers from New England to work with the slaves. Tubman knew she would be a useful link between the army and her people, so she said good-bye to her friends and family and arranged to go south. In May 1862, the governor of Massachusetts sent her to Beaufort, South Carolina, aboard the ship *Atlantic*.

At Beaufort, the commanding officer, Major General David Hunter, was very glad to see Tubman. His white soldiers and the freed slaves didn't understand each other. Tubman herself had problems at first. The slaves didn't know what to make of her until news spread that she had been a friend of John Brown's and a conductor on the Underground Railroad. Tubman and the freed slaves even spoke a different dialect. She said, "Why their language down here in the far South is just as different from ours in Maryland, as you can think. They laughed when they heard me talk, and I could not understand them."

There were other problems for Tubman. The contraband people resented the special way she was treated by the military, primarily because she ate the same food that the officers did. Tubman voluntarily gave up her rations and earned money to live on by making and selling pies and root beer. She worked for the government for over three years, but she received only $200 in pay. Most of that money went to build a washhouse, where she taught the contraband women to do laundry so they would be able to support themselves.

Tubman was one of many women who worked unofficially with Union troops. There was no organization of nurses during the Civil War. Both men and women, most without real training, helped care for the wounded. Although Governor Andrews of Massachusetts had sent her to South Carolina, Tubman had no official standing with the army. As a result, there were almost no army records to prove what she did for them.

It is known that at Hilton Head, South Carolina, Tubman looked after a primitive field hospital for contrabands. The refugees who streamed into the Union army camps had nothing but the tattered clothes they wore. Often they were half starved and sick from exposure. Sometimes they had been shot by Confederate soldiers. She nursed the sick and wounded back to health, but her care didn't stop there. She often tried to find work for them so they would be able to provide for themselves.

She also helped care for white soldiers. She later described her work as a nurse:

> I'd go to the hospital early every morning. I'd get a big chunk of ice, and put it in a basin, and fill it with water; then I'd take a sponge and begin. First man I'd come to, I'd thrash away the flies, and they'd rise, like bees round a hive. Then I'd begin to bathe the wounds, and by the time I'd bathed off three or four, the fire and heat would have melted the ice and made the water warm, and it would be as red as clear blood. Then I'd go and get more ice, and by the time I got back to the next ones, the flies would be round the first ones black and thick as ever.

Tubman was as fearless as a nurse as she had been as a conductor for the Underground Railroad. When the army sent her from Hilton Head, South Carolina, to a field hospital in Florida, she found both white soldiers and contrabands "dying off like sheep." She treated her patients with a medicine she made from roots. While in Florida, she cared for soldiers who had smallpox and other deadly diseases, but she never got any of the diseases herself. Her "special angel" was apparently still protecting her.

Harriet Tubman helped the white soldiers as gladly as she helped the contrabands, but she was especially proud to serve the African-American regiments. On January 1, 1863, Lincoln issued the Emancipation Proclamation. This freed the slaves in rebel states. He said the Union army would welcome them. Although Tubman was happy for the thousands of slaves who had been set free, she thought Lincoln's Emancipation Proclamation achieved too little and had come too late. Lincoln hadn't freed the slaves in the upper South, including those in her own state of Maryland, only those in the rebel states. Tubman thought that the real reason Lincoln emancipated the slaves was to strengthen the Union army.

The abolitionist Thomas Wentworth Higginson had come to South Carolina to lead the first African-American regiment made up of freed slaves. Colonel James Montgomery, who had ridden with John Brown in Kansas, was an expert on guerilla warfare. His African-American regiment carried on raids in the Charleston area, releasing slaves and terrorizing the enemy.

Tubman worked as a scout with Montgomery during the summer of 1863. She wasn't an ordinary scout, though. She put together a squad of spies, who kept Montgomery informed about slaves who might want to join the Union army. At night she would creep past Confederate outposts, into the country surrounding Charleston, South Carolina, and find out which slaves were ready to leave their masters. After she and her scouts had done the groundwork, she helped Montgomery plan the Combahee River raid. The purpose of the raid was to terrorize the whites and rescue freed slaves. Montgomery took three gunboats up the river, shelling the rebel outposts and gathering freed slaves aboard the boats.

One of the few firsthand accounts of the raid was that of a 73-year-old slave. He said that he had prayed all of his life to be free, then: "One day I look up, and I see a big cloud; it didn't come up like clouds come out far yonder, but it appeared to be right overhead. There was thunders out of that, and there was light-nings. Then I looked down on the water, and I see, appeared to me a big house in the water, and out of the big house came great big eggs, and the good eggs went on through the air, and fell into the fort; and the bad eggs burst before they got there." The old man watched the rebel troops run and hide in the swamp. "Then I heard it was the Yankee ship firing about those big eggs, and they had come to set us free." After a time, the slave realized that everything had become very quiet. "The birds stop flying, and the ravens stop crying, and when I go to catch a fish to eat with my rice, there's no fish there."

Tubman had a different view of the Combahee River raid:

We took away 756 head of their most valuable livestock. I never saw such a sight; we laughed, and laughed, and laughed. Here you'd see a woman with a pail on her head, rice a-smoking in it just as she'd taken it out from the fire, young one hanging on behind, one hand round her forehead to hold on, the other hand digging in the rice-pot, eating with all its might; hold of her dress two or three more; down her back a bag with a pig in it. One woman brought two pigs, a white one and a black one; we took them all on board; named the white pig Beauregard, and the black pig Jeff Davis. Sometimes the women would come with twins hanging round their necks; appears like I never saw so many twins in my life; bags on their shoulders, baskets on their heads, and young ones tagging behind, all loaded; pigs squealing, chickens screaming, young ones squalling.

Nearly all of the able-bodied men taken in the Combahee raid joined the Union army.

About a month after the raid, the July 10, 1863, issue of the Boston *Commonwealth* printed the following story:

HARRIET TUBMAN

Col. Montgomery and his gallant band of 300 black soldiers, under the guidance of a black woman, dashed into the enemy's country, struck a bold and effective blow, destroying millions of dollars worth of commissary stores, cotton and lordly dwellings, and striking terror into the heart of rebeldom, brought off near 800 slaves and thousands of dollars worth of property, without losing a man or receiving a scratch....

The article went on to say that before the raid, Tubman had risked her life time after time as she went behind the enemy lines on spying missions. Unfortunately, because she was not actually in the army, there are no records of those missions. She must have used her old tricks from the Underground Railroad to slip in and out of slave quarters like a shadow. Nineteen rescue trips as a conductor had taught her how to spot trustworthy people and get the information she needed. Then, as in the past, she picked her way back through enemy territory. She was probably no more afraid of the sharp-eyed rebel soldiers and their rifles than she had been of the slave catchers and their hounds.

Tubman's service to the army would soon come to an end, but before she left there was something she had to prove. Not everyone thought it was a good idea to use African Americans in combat. Some whites said black soldiers would run when the first shot was

A young escaped slave, barely in his teens, pictured at his induction into the Union Army.

The same young man in uniform, as a drummer for the Union Army.

A regiment of African-American Union Army soldiers poses for a group photograph.

fired. The Union paid them only half as much as it paid its white soldiers. Montgomery's soldiers had been used entirely for raids behind enemy lines, but the first large-scale battle using African-American troops against the Confederate army was led by Colonel Robert Gould Shaw.

Harriet Tubman proudly fixed the white colonel his last meal before battle. He and his troops were to take Fort Wagner, a fort that guarded the city of Charleston. His soldiers were northern African Americans and freed slaves who had volunteered for service. Shaw, leading the attack, climbed to the top of the fort and shouted to his men to follow. When the colonel was fatally wounded, many of his soldiers kept charging into the enemy fire. They knew they were doomed, but they also knew that if they turned back the world would call them cowards. Their bravery proved that African-American men could be fine soldiers.

After the battle, Harriet Tubman said, "And then we saw the lightning, and that was the guns; and then we heard the thunder, and that was the *big* guns; and then we heard the rain falling, and that was the drops of blood falling; and when we came to get in the crops, it was dead men that we reaped."

REWARDS

"Most that I have done has been in public, and I
have received much encouragement.... You on
the other hand have labored in a private way.... I
have had the applause of the crowd.... While
most that you have done has been witnessed by a
few trembling, scared, and footsore
bondmen.... The midnight sky and the silent
stars have been the witnesses of your devotion to
freedom and of your heroism."

FREDERICK DOUGLASS

In 1864, Harriet Tubman returned to her home in Auburn,
New York. Her parents needed her, and she was exhausted
after three years of war. Her sleeping spells had become
more frequent and she, like other veterans of war, could not get the
horror out of her mind. As if this weren't enough, and in spite of
her service to the Union and all the kind words that had been
written about her, she was penniless. She carried with her pieces of
paper she couldn't read—travel passes and letters of praise from
officers she had served—but she had no money to live on.

The army paid a bounty, or reward, to people who recruited
African Americans. It owed Tubman at least $1,800 for her work at
Combahee, but it refused to pay. Long afterward, a writer for the
New York Herald wrote: "It is one of the greatest injustices of the
war that, although Harriet was promised the regular bounty then
offered for recruits, she never received a dollar for bringing about
this wholesale enlistment."

An African-American abolitionist in Boston, who had recruited
soldiers for Shaw's regiment, tried to get help for Tubman. He
placed an article in the *Commonwealth* asking for donations of

money and clothing. At this time Tubman met Sojourner Truth, another powerful African-American woman who fought for abolition. Truth was on her way to visit President Lincoln to thank him for all he had done for African-American people. Tubman didn't understand why Sojourner Truth wanted to thank the president because she had never thought of Lincoln as a friend of her people. She blamed him for not paying the African-American soldiers what they deserved. She still thought the only reason he had freed the slaves was to build up his armies, not to destroy slavery. Later Tubman changed her mind about Lincoln, but he was never a hero to her the way John Brown had been.

In February 1865, Lincoln decided to create an all-black army, using black instead of white officers. This was the idea of Martin Delany, the African-American physician, explorer, and abolitionist publisher. Word had reached the North that the Confederacy was about to arm its slaves and send them to fight the Union. Delany wanted to use the old Underground Railroad to warn the slaves and bring them out of the South before such a thing happened. These slaves could then serve in the all-black army. Delany rounded up African-American leaders for the army, including Harriet Tubman. He arranged for her trip back to Charleston, where she would work as a scout. Instead of going directly to South Carolina, however, Tubman went to Fortress Monroe, in Virginia, where she had heard there was a great need for nurses.

At Fortress Monroe, she found terrible conditions and decided to ask some of her powerful friends for help. The war ended on April 9, 1865, very soon after Tubman arrived in Virginia. She then went to Washington, where she visited her good friend William Seward, Lincoln's secretary of state. She told him about the needs of the contraband hospital at Fortress Monroe. Seward tried to get her appointed as nurse and matron at Fortress Monroe. He also tried to get the army to pay her some of the money it already owed her. Nothing came of Seward's efforts, nor of Delany's plan for an all-black army. Once again, Tubman headed home to Auburn, empty-handed.

On her way home, Tubman carried a pass identifying her as a hospital nurse. This entitled her to half fare on the train. Because she couldn't read train schedules, Tubman usually just went to the train station and got on whatever train seemed to be going in the right direction. This time she got on the wrong train. When the conductor asked for her ticket, she showed him her pass. He called her a name and told her that African Americans could not ride for half fare. She tried to explain that she was traveling on the same kind of pass that soldiers were given.

The conductor grabbed her arm and twisted it, saying, "I'll make you tired of staying here." Three men came and helped the conductor throw Tubman into the baggage car, where she stayed until the train reached New York.

After her return to Auburn, Tubman kept trying to get the money the government owed her. She needed this money for herself and her aged parents, but she also needed it for all the poverty-stricken freed slaves who showed up at her front door in need of food and shelter. Right after the war, she got money from many abolitionist friends. Seward had even helped her buy the house in which she and her parents lived.

Tubman might have been able to get along during those postwar years if she had been willing to sit back and putter in her garden. She had a house and a place to raise vegetables. Her neighbors in Auburn were very proud of her. But her life's work wasn't over. If she got her hands on a little bit of money, she sent it off to support schools for freedmen in the South. She planned to start a home for the aged as soon as the government paid her.

Tubman had also become involved in a new battle for human equality. She agreed with Sojourner Truth, Susan B. Anthony, and Elizabeth Cady Stanton in their efforts to advance the rights of women. With them and all the other abolitionists, she was overjoyed when the 13th Amendment to the Constitution finally outlawed slavery throughout the United States. She was also happy when the 14th Amendment made it unlawful to have one set of laws for white people and another for blacks, or to keep people from earning a living or going to school because of their color. She probably hoped the 14th Amendment would put an end to the practice of Jim Crow. She hoped it meant that African-American passengers would never again be forced from seats they had paid to sit in.

Tubman remained devoted to Susan B. Anthony even when Anthony split with such old abolitionist friends as Frederick Douglass. Anthony believed that the time had come to work for women's rights. It angered her when the 15th Amendment gave black men, but neither black nor white women, the right to vote. This upset Tubman, too. When she was asked many years later if she thought women should have the right to vote, she answered, "I suffered enough to believe it."

Douglass thought women should be allowed to vote, but he believed that racism was a much more urgent issue. He was very angry with Anthony for starting the suffragist, or women's rights, movement in 1870. He and many other abolitionists thought Anthony's action weakened the African Americans' battle for equality. He said that women should wait—that after people of color were truly free, there would be time to work for women's rights.

Tubman attended most suffragist meetings that were held in the Auburn area. She may have suspected that she was having such a hard time getting her money from the government more because she was a woman than because she was African American. The African-American men who had served in the army for half pay had sued for back wages and had gotten them. Yet even with letters from Seward, and long, documented accounts of her services, the army and Congress ignored her request.

In 1867, Tubman's friend Sarah Bradford wrote a short biography of her life. She hoped to raise money for Tubman through the sale of the book and by calling attention to her accomplishments. Bradford wrote from testimonials from Tubman's friends. She included many in her book, but Frederick Douglass's letter addressed to Tubman was the most eloquent. Douglass began by saying how glad he was that she was finally getting some recognition. He said:

> The difference between us is very marked. Most that I have done and suffered in the service of our cause has been in public, and I have received much encouragement at every step of the way. You, on the other hand, have labored in a private way. I have wrought in the day—you at night. I have had the applause of the crowd and the satisfaction that comes with being approved by the multitude, while most that you have done has been witnessed by a few trembling, scarred, and footsore bondmen and women, whom you have led out of the house of bondage, and whose heartfelt *"God bless you"* has been your only reward.

Bradford's book earned $1,200 for Tubman, but the money was gone almost as soon as it had come. Tubman's use for large sums of money had always been to help those who couldn't help themselves. Some people believed she behaved foolishly and thought this was a sign that she couldn't handle money. Tubman wanted to start a home for the poor and aged because there was a great need. If the North had not welcomed its African-American workers, it certainly did not want those African Americans who could no longer work. When she brought her own parents North, she had received harsh criticism from proslavery people. In the plantation system, slaves who were too old to work were fed, clothed, and sheltered for the rest of their lives. In the North, they often became dependent on charity. All her life Tubman accepted the responsibility for making changes. If she had any way at all of doing what needed to be done, she did it.

Tubman never got her back pay, but she did finally get a pension. In 1869, she married Nelson Davis, a younger man who had fought in the Civil War. He was in poor health and probably suffered from tuberculosis. Harriet took care of him for many years. Not long after his death in 1888, Congress passed the Pension Act for widows of Civil War veterans. Tubman was awarded an $8-

Harriet Tubman escaped slavery and abuse to lead her folk to freedom on the Underground Railroad.

a-month pension for her late husband's service. Ten years later, when she was 77 years old, her friends tried to get the pension increased to $25, based on her own record of service in the army. After the representative from her district received a petition signed by the most prominent citizens of Auburn, he put a bill before Congress for the larger pension. An act of Congress increased Tubman's widow's pension to $20, but she still received no official recognition for her own remarkable service.

Even at the age of 75, Tubman still wasn't ready to retire. For several years, she had been looking at 25 acres of land that was next to her own property. It was just what she needed for the cooperative farm she had always hoped to give to her poor. In 1896, she heard that the land was to be auctioned off. With very little money in her pocket, she went to the auction. Describing the scene later, she said: "They were all white folks but me there, and there I was like a blackberry in a pail of milk, but I hid down in a corner, and no one knew who was bidding." Other people wanted the land, too, so the bids went higher and higher. Tubman's bid of $1,450 won. She didn't have the money, but she knew the bank would lend it to her.

Tubman finally had the place she needed. Able-bodied people with no money would be able to work on the farm. People who were too old to work would have the food and shelter they needed. It wasn't quite that easy, though. She had the bank payments to make and a great deal of hard work. Her years of hotel work had prepared her for cooking; her war experience had prepared her for the nursing. But she was too old to manage the place by herself. In 1903, when she was in her eighties, she gave ownership of the farm to the African Methodist Episcopal Zion Church. The church formally opened the home in 1908. Tubman wanted it called the John Brown Home, but the Zion Church called it the Harriet Tubman Home. She wanted both black and white leaders on its board of directors. The church wanted only people of color. She wanted the home to be completely free, but the church charged $100 a year. She didn't want to have anything to do with running the home after that.

Tubman spent the last two years of her life at the home she had founded. She received visitors, but she was too weak to get around. She had outlived nearly all of the great abolitionists. Garrison had died long ago. She had gone to Wendell Phillips's funeral. A few years later, she went to the funeral of Frederick Douglass. Thomas Garrett was gone. William Still. Gerrit Smith.

On March 10, 1913, surrounded by friends softly singing "Swing Low, Sweet Chariot," Harriet Tubman died.

The Auburn post of the Grand Army of the Republic gave her a military funeral. If the Union army had not recognized her value, at least its veterans had. A year later, the citizens of Auburn set aside a day to celebrate the life of Harriet Tubman. Flags flew, Booker T. Washington, the famous African-American educator, made a speech, and the town dedicated a memorial to Harriet Tubman— the Moses of her People.

TIMETABLE OF EVENTS IN THE LIFE OF
HARRIET TUBMAN

1820 or
1821   Born in Dorchester County, Maryland. Named Araminta.

1827   Goes to work for Miss Susan, who whips her so badly she is scarred for life

1831   Takes the name Harriet. Nat Turner's insurrection is put down in Southampton County, Virginia.

1844   Marries John Tubman

1849   Escapes to Pennsylvania through the Underground Railroad

1850   Begins work with Underground Railroad. Rescues family. The Fugitive Slave Law is passed.

1851   Rescues one of her brothers, his wife, and nine others.

1852   Brings brother and other fugitives to St. Catharines in Canada. *Uncle Tom's Cabin* is published.

1854   Rescues two brothers and three others from Thompson's plantation in Maryland on Christmas Eve

1857   Rescues parents and brings them to Auburn, New York

1858   Meets John Brown in St. Catharines and supports his plan to attack Harpers Ferry

1860   Speaks to white audience in Boston. After 18 trips along Underground Railroad, makes final rescue in December

1862   Works as nurse for Union army in Beaufort, South Carolina

1863   Becomes a Union spy and performs several successful raids and scouting missions. Emancipation Proclamation becomes effective.

1865   Civil War ends. U.S. Government refuses to pay Tubman for time served with Union army.

1867   Sarah Bradford's biography of Tubman is published.

1869   Marries Nelson Davis

1870   Supports Susan B. Anthony in founding women's suffragist movement

1888   Nelson Davis dies.

1908   Harriet Tubman Home opens.

1913   Dies March 10

Suggested Reading

*Bains, Rae. *Harriet Tubman: The Road to Freedom*. Mahwah, N.J.: Troll, 1982.

Birney, Catherine H. *The Grimké Sisters*. 1885. Reprint. Westport, Conn.: Greenwood, 1969.

*Buckmaster, Henrietta. *Flight to Freedom*. New York: Crowell, 1958.

*Childress, Alice. *When the Rattlesnake Sounds*. New York: Coward, 1975.

*Epstein, Sam and Beryl. *Harriet Tubman: Guide to Freedom*. Champaign, Ill.: Garrard, 1968.

*Ferris, Jeri. *Go Free or Die: A Story About Harriet Tubman*. Minneapolis: Lerner Publications, 1989.

*McGovern, Ann. *Runaway Slave: The Story of Harriet Tubman*. New York: Four Winds, 1965.

*Petry, Ann. *Harriet Tubman: Conductor on the Underground Railroad*. New York: Crowell, 1955.

Scott, John Anthony. *Woman Against Slavery*. New York: Crowell, 1978.

*Sterling, Dorothy. *Freedom Train: The Story of Harriet Tubman*. New York: Scholastic, 1954.

*Sterling, Philip, and Rayford Logan. *Four Took Freedom*. Garden City, N.Y.: Zenith, 1967.

Still, William. *The Underground Railroad*. 1872. Reprint. New York: Arno, 1968.

*White, Terry Anne. *North to Liberty: The Story of the Underground Railroad*. Champaign, Ill.: Garrard, 1972.

*Readers of *Harriet Tubman: Slavery and the Underground Railroad* will find these books particularly readable.

SELECTED SOURCES

Bancroft, Frederic. *Slave-Trading in the Old South*. Baltimore: Furst, 1931.

Blassingame, John W. *The Slave Community: Plantation Life in the Ante-Bellum South*. New York: Oxford University Press, 1972.

Blockson, Charles S. "The Underground Railroad." *National Geographic*. July 1984: pp.3–39.

Bowley, Harkless. Letter to Earl Conrad. August 8, 1939.

Bracket, Jeffrey C. *The Negro in Maryland*. Baltimore: Johns Hopkins University, 1889.

Bradford, Sarah H. *Scenes in the Life of Harriet Tubman*. 1869. Reprint. Secaucus, N.J.: Citadel, 1961.

Campbell, Penelope. *Maryland in Africa*. Urbana: University of Illinois Press, 1971.

Conrad, Earl. *Harriet Tubman*. 1943. Reprint. New York: Eriksson, 1969.

Douglass, Frederick. *My Bondage and My Freedom*. 1855. Reprint. New York: Arno, 1968.

Foner, Philip S. *Frederick Douglass*. New York: Citadel, 1969.

Garrison, William Lloyd. *The New "Reign of Terror" in the Slaveholding States*. 1860. Reprint. New York: Arno, 1969.

Gates, Henry Louis, Jr. *Six Women's Slave Narratives*. New York: Oxford University Press, 1988.

Hinton, Richard J. *John Brown and His Men*. 1894. Reprint. New York: Arno, 1968.

Kemble, Frances Anne. *Journal of a Residence on a Georgia Plantation*. London: Longman, 1863.

Lay My Burden Down: A Folk History of Slavery. Chicago: University of Chicago Press, 1945.

Mannix, Daniel P., and Malcolm Cowley. *Black Cargoes*. New York: Viking, 1962.

Nye, Russel B. *William Lloyd Garrison and the Humanitarian Reformers*. Boston: Little, Brown, 1955.

Olmsted, Frederick Law. *A Journey in the Seaboard Slave States*. 1856. Reprint. New York: Negro Universities Press, 1968.

Rawley, James A. *The Transatlantic Slave Trade*. New York: Norton, 1981.

Ripley, C. Peter, ed. *The Black Abolitionist Papers, Vol. I.* Chapel Hill: University of North Carolina Press, 1985.

Rose, Willie Lee. *A Documentary History of Slavery in North America*. New York: Oxford University Press, 1976.

Siebert, Wilbur Henry. *The Underground Railroad*. 1898. Reprint. New York: Arno, 1968.

Stamp, Kenneth M. *The Peculiar Institution*. New York: Vintage, 1956.

Stephenson, H. *Isaac Franklin, Slave Trader and Planter of the Old South*. Birmingham: University of Alabama Press, 1938.

Still, William. *The Underground Railroad*. 1872. Reprint. New York: Arno, 1968.

Stoddard, Hope. *Famous American Women*. New York: Crowell, 1970.

Stowe, Harriet Beecher. *Writings of Harriet Beecher Stowe, Volume II: Uncle Tom's Cabin* and *A Key to Uncle Tom's Cabin*. 1852, 1853. Reprint. New York: AMS, 1967.

Stowe, Harriet Beecher. *The Life of Harriet Beecher Stowe*. Ed. Charles Edward Stowe. 1889. Reprint. Detroit: Gale, 1967.

Webb, Richard D., ed. *Life and Letters of Captain John Brown*. 1861. Reprint. Westport, Conn.: Negro Universities Press, 1972.

Wish, Harvey. *Slavery in the South*. New York: Noonday, 1964.

Yetman, Norman. *Voices from Slavery*. New York: Holt, 1970.

INDEX

Vigilance Committee, 65

Washington, Booker T., 124
Webster, Daniel, 38
Weld, Theodore, 93, 94

Western Female Institute, 93
Wilson, Hiram, 82

Zong (ship), 18

PICTURE CREDITS

Megan McClard is an associate professor of English at Metropolitan State College in Denver, where for the past fourteen years she has taught writing and women's studies. She has also taught writing at Eastern Montana College and the University of Denver, where she received her Ph.D. in English. She writes adult fiction, juvenile fiction, and biography for young adults, including a biography of Hiawatha.